# MY KIDS
# PLAY HOCKEY

# MY KIDS PLAY HOCKEY

## ESSENTIAL ADVICE FOR EVERY HOCKEY PARENT

### CHRISTIE CASCIANO BURNS

SPORTS
PUBLISHING

Sports Publishing books may be purchased in bulk at special discounts for sales promotion, corporate gifts, fund-raising, or educational purposes. Special editions can also be created to specifications. For details, contact the Special Sales Department, Sports Publishing, 307 West 36th Street, 11th Floor, New York, NY 10018 or sportspubbooks@skyhorsepublishing.com.

Sports Publishing® is a registered trademark of Skyhorse Publishing, Inc.®, a Delaware corporation.

Visit our website at www.sportspubbooks.com.

10 9 8 7 6 5 4 3 2 1

Library of Congress Cataloging-in-Publication Data is available on file.

Cover design by Tom Lau
Cover photo credit: Jim Lamanna

ISBN: 978-1-683581-79-6
Ebook ISBN: 978-1-683581-80-2

Printed in China

# CONTENTS

# FOREWORD

**A**s he travels around Minnesota, the "State of Hockey," people like to say that University of Minnesota Head Coach Don Lucia has the best job in hockey. He's quick to correct that perception.

"I have the second-best job in hockey," he says. "The first is being the head coach at an orphanage: no parents to deal with."

It's a punchline that usually brings down the house on the hockey-banquet circuit.

Poor hockey parents. From late-night comics to daily newspaper columnists, for too long they've been the butt of the joke. All they do is drive kids to and from the rink, spend hours drinking bad vending machine coffee on frigid metal bleachers, giving up their nights and weekends while devoting huge sums of the family budget to equipment, ice time, and sports drinks. And this is the thanks they get.

There's no doubt that their hearts are in the right place. Sometimes it takes a nudge to get their brains to follow suit. For that we have Christie Casciano Burns.

For the past four years, Christie's monthly "Hockey Mom" columns have been required reading for the 425,000 readers of *USA Hockey Magazine*. Drawing on her twenty years in the youth hockey trenches, she brings a wit and wisdom that comes with spending countless hours in the rink, while mixing in a little cutting humor and good, old-fashioned motherly advice that speaks to and for grizzled veterans and newcomers to the sport alike.

*My Kids Play Hockey* is a compilation of Christie's work that has appeared in the pages of *USA Hockey Magazine* over the years. Whether your kid shoots a puck, kicks a soccer ball, or swings a baseball bat, her sound and sage advice is required reading for all sports parents. Because when it comes to keeping your head in the game, this mother definitely knows best.

—Harry Thompson, *USA Hockey Magazine*

# INTRODUCTION

**W**hen the call came, it was like winning my own personal Stanley Cup championship! At the other end of the line was Harry Thompson, editor of *USA Hockey Magazine*. Membership in USA Hockey brings with it a subscription to the hockey world's most widely circulated magazine. On days when the latest issue came, my kids couldn't wait to get home from school so they could read about their favorite players and pore over ads for all the latest gear. It's no stretch to say the magazine holds rock star status in our house . . . and the editor was calling for me!

Harry was looking for someone to write a monthly column from the perspective of a "Mom in the Trenches." At that point in my life, I was a mom . . . and I was fully entrenched in all things hockey, meaning that I was a perfect fit.

We had youth hockey players in our family. And, as any hockey parent knows, youth hockey can consume your life. It's not a sport for the faint of heart. It changes the way your family eats, travels, communicates, and vacations. With two hockey players in our lives, the sport became the answer to so many questions from friends and extended family:

How come you never come over for dinner on the weekend? "My kids play hockey."

Why on Earth did you get an SUV? "My kids play hockey."

You've only had that SUV for a year. How did you ever pile up so many miles in so little time? "My kids play hockey."

On empty again? Didn't you just fill up that gas tank?

Do I even need to tell you the answer? You get the picture. And now, you get the title!

Looking back at my first year as a full-fledged hockey mom, I was pretty overwhelmed. Fortunately, I had a lot of help along the way. At the time, my husband was a detective sergeant with the Syracuse Police Department. He was working nights, and spending many hours on a lengthy undercover investigation. That kept him working nearly non-stop during my son's entire first year of hockey. I was also working full-time as morning news anchor at WSYR TV. My shift would end just as my husband would head into work. I was left trekking from one unheated rink to another with our young son, with our baby girl in my arms.

We are an active and athletic family, but my husband never played hockey, and my time on the rink occurred as a figure skater. Prior to putting him on the ice, we introduced our son to just about every sport on the planet, but none of them stuck. Finally, we put a stick in his hands and skates on his feet. Wouldn't you know, he'd pick the one sport we knew nothing about? Or more likely, the sport picked him.

As soon as I sat in our first meeting for hockey parents, I knew I was entering a brave new world. It was a little like dropping into a foreign country, with a new language to learn and a whole new culture to embrace. Our family life was clearly about to change. Being a hockey parent is different than any other role in sports. It is a big responsibility. At times, you may regret that your kids found their fiery passion on a frozen tundra. But the hockey world has its benefits. It is a tight-knit community that gives back to those who open their hearts to the game. While they are on the ice, your kids grow in ways you never imagined possible. And, it turns out, they aren't the only ones who skate away with life lessons.

Learning the hockey basics was a real challenge for me. I had to figure out everything from the meaning of offside to the secret to lacing up a hockey skate. (I always had a tough time lacing my son's skates tight enough, until another hockey mom taught me the trick of lacing up with a skate key. Problem solved.) I also had to learn how to handle unexpected equipment snafus, like when a skate blade snaps right before a crucial tournament game. I also learned very quickly why it's so important to get wet gear out of the bag as soon as your home, if you expect to have any chance of keeping the stench to a tolerable level.

There was much to figure out. There were the basics, like preparing meals ahead of time, knowing how to budget, and dressing for a long, cold season. Some of these lessons came at a price. I blew out my hair dryer trying to thaw my frozen feet after enduring one my first games on the metal bleachers in an unheated rink. Sneakers without socks may look good, but believe me . . . they are "too cool" for your own good. Another lesson learned: if you lay out the money for one of those wheeled hockey bags, pick them up when you go across the parking lot or the salt and ice-fighting chemicals will eat a hole in the bottom of your bag. We didn't figure that out until it was too late, and I lost a neck guard somewhere in the middle of a seemingly endless Buffalo parking lot.

Fortunately, in those early years, there were many generous and willing hockey parents who eagerly stepped up to share their experience with this very clueless mom.

My *USA Hockey Magazine* column made its debut in September of 2013. With Harry's coaching on topic selection, we've covered everything from how to organize your hockey household, successful fundraising strategies, and even a column titled, "Oh Behave! How to Act like an Adult at a Youth Hockey Game." That column could have reached epic proportions.

Once the columns got rolling, feedback started pouring in. I've gotten messages through social media from hockey parents around the country, sharing advice and ideas and always willing to add perspective on the sport, how it's impacted their family, and even offering suggestions for future hockey mom topics. Since it's been so well received, we thought why not put it all in book form and give it some shelf life?

Our goal is to share usable knowledge and experiences from real experts on the subject, hockey parents who have been there, done that, and finally gotten it right. Oh, the things I wish I'd known when I was starting out . . . and the time and money I could have saved! I hope you'll think of the following pages as a crash course, akin to Hacks for Hockey Parents, with tips and tricks that might make your entry into this world just a little bit easier and saner.

I have been truly blessed by my family's experiences, and the bond that hockey has helped forge with my children. And over the last few years, these columns have connected me with other passionate hockey parents. Like me, they've been willing to put their advice and experience down on paper. In this book, you'll benefit from real voices of reason from some of my favorite hockey parents and bloggers. Kevin Duy, Mark Gilman, Bill Cahill, Sharon Enck, Caroline Stanistreet, and Diane Pelton all add advice that is priceless. Writing about the sport has enhanced our lives and been incredibly rewarding work. Our goal is to help develop good hockey players who are also good people and provide good guidance for families as they get ready to start on this fabulous journey. Happy Hockey Trails to you!

# 1

# BACK TO HOCKEY, BACK TO SCHOOL

## The Season Could be a Blockbuster Hit or Total Bust Depending on Your Directorial Skills

The curtain is about to open on a new hockey season, and as your family's director, you're hoping for a good show with no drama. While you can't control the actions of the entire cast of characters, you can take some cues from veteran hockey parents to successfully produce a season that will draw rave reviews. So take the following cues and get ready for an action-packed thriller that hopefully will generate very little drama.

### Setting the Stage

Get organized. Find a place in your house for all things hockey. The area needs to be functional with room for all your players' gear. A good drying rack and hooks to hang bags and sticks will help reduce clutter. Get your kids into a routine of hanging up their gear as soon as they get home from a practice or game. If you want to cut down on the hockey bag stench, don't allow the equipment to fester inside the bag. Ever. I speak here from experience.

Marking your schedule on a big calendar placed in a strategic spot in your house will let everyone know when it's show time and to help avoid conflicts with other main events. My family personally prefers a dry-erase board. True, they are about as old school as it gets, but it's been a great way for our family to see, at a glance, where we need to be and when. For the more modern family, there are an assortment of free apps that allow easy access to your calendar from your electronic devices that can be shared with other family members. Use whatever works best for you.

### The Dress Rehearsal

Have your hockey player try on all the gear before the season starts, from head to toe. Don't jeopardize your child's ability to play or their safety with equipment that is too small, too tight, or too big.

"When kids are younger, ill-fitting equipment can be traumatic," says Mark Gilman, Michigan hockey dad of three boys and owner and general manager of the Motor City Hawks junior team of the United States Premier Hockey League, or USPHL.

"I've witnessed over the years with many youth players coming to the bench crying because their shin guards, shoulder pads, or gloves were either hurting them or rubbing the wrong way."

Syracuse sports shop owner and coach Dave McKie says that typically, girls stop growing out of their skates at age thirteen, and boys at age fifteen.

"After those years, check for skates that are worn out. Skates should normally last two seasons and at least fifty games a season.

Check skate blades often. When bent or worn down by sharpening, they can negatively affect skating," McKie says. He also suggests replacing the steel as a less expensive option to buying new skates.

Gilman adds that every parent wants to save money, but the helmet is the last thing you need to skimp on. "I've seen parents spend a lot of money on the top-of-the-line shin guards, gloves, and sticks," he says. "But after watching one of my sons suffer a concussion a few seasons ago, I realized very quickly that the most important investment I could make was to purchase the best [most protective] helmet I could find."

### *Financial Backing*

We all know that hockey can be an expensive production. It's best to budget and set aside money for the unexpected.

When the registration email lands in the inbox for Camillus, New York, travel hockey dad Bill Huba, his first thought is to get out the checkbook. "First, the bite of registration, then the sting of new equipment," he says. "Then you look forward to an extra five thousand miles on the minivan driving to practices and games, plus hotels, meals, tourney fees, etc. It's a part of the landscape of suffering we endure as hockey parents hoping for a few seconds of absolute joy when your kid touches the puck and does something great."

Gilman, who has watched his three sons play hockey over the past seventeen years, says parents should be given a complete budget, before the season starts. "It's impossible to budget without one, and it brings accountability to your team. It also cuts down on surprises later," he says. "Some parents feel it's not their role to ask for these, and I've never understood that.

It's your money and you should have a very clear and succinct written budget showing you how that money is being spent and what the season's financial expectations are."

### Taking the Show on the Road

Pittsburgh's Dana Vento, mother of two hockey players, knows how travel and tournaments can really ice the budget.

Before they hit the road, Vento always plans ahead by packing appropriate snacks, sandwiches, and drinks. It's the kind of planning that helps her family avoid the lure of the drive thru.

"Google the areas around you before you travel there and check for apps that save you money for anything from food purchases to shopping," Vento says. "Don't forget to check with AAA for discounted, clean lodging and consider a credit card that will earn you cash back every time you spend. These small steps save hundreds of dollars a year, enough to pay for gas or new skates."

Team potluck dinners at the hotel can also be a cheaper alternative to a local restaurant and a great way to bond as a team.

### Intermission

School comes first. With the right guidance, your children will become pros at balancing a busy school schedule in addition to sports, other extracurricular activities, and family obligations. But set rules and stick to them.

"One of the balancing acts for us has always been scheduling homework around practices," Gilman says. "Our kids know that if it's not done before, they don't go and may suffer the consequences with their coaches.

"Allowing them to do homework after practice or a game is a bad idea. They're tired and won't put their full effort into it.

Also, many times they plead to get up early and do it in the morning. This doesn't work either."

The guilt trip kicks in when kids miss school for tournaments. Gilman says sharing your hockey schedule with teachers is a good way to recruit a valuable ally.

"It's imperative to get the teachers your kid's tournament schedule at the beginning of the school year so they can plan accordingly," he says. "Also remind them by email a week ahead. Teachers understand these commitments and will, in almost all cases, make sure necessary homework or tests that might be missed are rescheduled earlier or when they return. They are less than cooperative if you tell them at the last minute."

### Take Five
Carve out time in your busy schedule for family time.

Oswego, New York, hockey coach and parent Bill Cahill says, "When I am the head coach, I always give the week of Christmas off and I try not to schedule long trips around Thanksgiving or New Years as well.

"I also feel it is the parents' obligation to say no, when asked for input by coaches, or their own kids request to go to an extra tournament with some other team. Staying home on a Sunday and having a home-cooked meal around a kitchen table is always a good thing."

### The Cast and Crew (Find Your Role)
It takes a team to run a team. From volunteering to serve as team organizer, to offering to coordinate the team's fundraisers, to being the parent who oversees locker room snacks, you don't have to take on a starring role, but the coach will certainly

appreciate any and all assists from parents. A preseason meeting can help set the tone for team obligations, explore coaching philosophy, and share input if the season's early draft needs revisions.

"In all the years I've been involved in youth hockey, the one thing I can point to with certainty each year is that the parents who complain the most during the season are usually the ones who fail to volunteer for anything," Gilman says. "Your perspective changes greatly when you're helping with fundraisers, scheduling, team trips, etc."

## Marquee Performance

Selflessness and sacrifice should be recurring themes. Impress upon your son or daughter the importance of passing the puck with the reminder that a real star makes everyone shine. If at the end of the show your star has made it through the season injury-free, experienced personal development, and most of all had fun, then you can call it a hit. All that's left is to roll the credits, take a bow, and hope for an encore next season.

Joe, Christie, and Sophia gearing up for another hockey season. Photo by Jim Lamanna

# 2

## YOU BETTER SHOP AROUND FOR THE RIGHT TEAM

There's some things that I want you to know
Just as sure as the wind's gonna blow
Hockey teams come and hockey teams gonna go
Before you tell 'em that you love 'em so
This hockey mama is telling you–
You better shop around.

Had Smokey Robinson been a hockey parent, he'd probably be singing a similar tune.

While this particular ditty may be cute, you're probably thinking it makes no sense since teams pick kids, not the other way around. Not necessarily.

If your young hockey player enjoys playing multiple sports and participating in other activities during the season, you'll want to find a program that will give them a chance to develop their skills and still have time to be a kid.

Before you sign your son or daughter up for the "A" team, make sure you ask the "C" question: commitment.

"As a parent you need to know start of the season, end of the season, holiday schedule, and weekly commitment," says North Salem, New York, hockey dad and coach Michael Bonelli, who also advises parents to size up the coach.

"If you choose to play for a team and a coach that offers little to no flexibility when it comes to other activities, then you're setting yourself up for frustration before the season even begins."

Bonelli says the top teams may not always be the best fit.

Commitment is huge. Be honest about what you can do and what you can afford. If you feel that 6 a.m. weekday practices will jeopardize grades, attitude, and strain your family life, then maybe you should pass on that team.

Ask lots of questions before signing on the dotted line. Do all players play every position, or is the coach going to determine your child is a "born defenseman" at age nine? Do you still have to pay if you don't make all of the tournaments? Do all the kids have to buy yet another warm-up jacket and pants? Can your child also be in the school musical? It's better to find out early on before it's too late.

Finding a good match may take a little extra work, but is well worth the effort.

"Finding a team, a coach, and an organization that adheres to the same values and expectations as your family will make for a smoother experience throughout the season," Bonelli says.

While you might not find a team that fits as snugly as a comfortable pair of old Super Tacks, getting answers to your questions can make for a happy and rewarding season for everyone involved.

# 3

## TODAY'S QUESTIONS CAN SAVE ON HEADACHES AND HEARTBURN TOMORROW

**H**ockey is a sport that demands toughness from its players. As parents, we don't question that requirement, but sometimes we forget that our little gladiators are still children.

Here's a case in point: Hockey dad Mark Gilman noticed that his son was cranky and his grades were slipping. Could his diet have been off? Was there some kind of problem at school? It turns out that hockey was the likely culprit.

While the season was great, the practice times were less than ideal. Gilman says the schedule took its toll on his thirteen-year-old son, depriving him of necessary sleep with ice times that didn't end until 10:30 p.m. on some school nights.

"If we had been part of the decision-making [process] early on, asking questions and balking as a parent group, it probably wouldn't have happened," Gilman says. "We should have asked more questions."

Finances can be another important factor. As a hockey dad, Gilman has seen money wasted on expensive uniforms, travel commitments, and prime ice times that could have been shared with other teams.

"Of course, there are a lot of teams that never give out financials, and these are teams to stay clear of," Gilman says. "It's your money and you have the right to know where it's going."

It's also important to know about a coach's philosophy heading into the season. Is he looking to develop your son or daughter as a player and a person, or simply win a league championship?

Knowing the coach's attitude is key, according to Jamie McKinven, former professional hockey player and author of the book, *So You Want Your Kid to Play Pro Hockey?*

"It is also important to be leery of coaches who promise things," McKinven says. "For example, coaches who promise that your kid will get drafted are hockey's version of a shady used car salesman."

Also important is to have realistic expectations when it comes to elite travel teams, cautions longtime hockey coach Vincent Stanley, Jr. "There is no correlation to the money you spend on your child's athletic elite travel team and their ability to play at a higher level," Stanley says. "You can't buy talent."

So before your hockey player suits up for another season, do your homework and ask plenty of questions to make sure both the team and the association suit your family.

# 4

## HOW TO MAKE TRYOUTS LESS STRESSFUL

**Tryout time can** be a trying period for parents and kids. There will be drama. There will be stress. (There might be even enough of it to go around for a new reality TV series, slide over *Dance Moms*, think "*Hockey Moms*"!) But parents should remove themselves from the drama and step into the arena with only positive words and actions. As badly as you want your kids to make the team, remember, it's not about you. Dealing with disappointing you, on top of the disappointment of not making the team, can be a lot for a child to handle. So your job is to be upbeat before, during, and after evaluations and tryouts. The message should be, do your best, but if you don't make it, you'll find something else, maybe something better. Staying out of the coach's face and staying out of your kid's head could just give your hockey player the edge and certainly will take the edge off of tryouts.

What about practice? It's important, but don't push it. Practice only as much as they can handle, because you certainly don't want to burn them out on the sport before the season begins. Make sure you do a thorough equipment check; everything needs to feel right and fit right. For knowing what to expect, and how best to impress, I turned to a well-respected West Genesee (New York) high school hockey coach, whose teams have earned state title championships. Frank Colabufo has been part of the player evaluations and selection process for twenty-five seasons. Here are his thoughts for players and parents for tryouts:

## Knowing How to Make a Team
### *Leave No Doubt*

As a player, you need to have the mindset that it is your job to make the team, not the coach's job to pick you. You need to separate yourself from the rest of the group. If you don't, you risk being "on the bubble" and it may end up bursting at the end of the tryout. Here are a few ways to give yourself the best shot at making a team.

### *Fly*

Play fast! Keep your feet moving and play with energy. Be strong in traffic and along the wall.

### *Win the Little Battles*

Win every one-on-one battle all over the ice. Have a constant work ethic in every drill and on every shift. Get loose pucks first and play with an edge. Be hard to play against. Take it personally and never give up.

### *Play off the Puck*

Research shows the best players in the world only possess the puck for about one minute in a sixty-minute game. So what are you doing when you don't have the puck? Support the play on both offense and defense. Stay engaged and make a difference.

### *Character Matters*

Be a positive team player. Make your teammates better players. Be willing to accept a role. The third line center that won't be happy unless she is on the first power play unit probably gets cut. Carry your own bag and sticks even if your parent offers to carry them for you. Say "please" and "thank you" when you get a drink from the snack bar after practice. Do the right thing, even when you think nobody is looking. I have had teams that have won championships with players that were less talented, but I've never won a championship with teams that lacked character.

## Keeping Your Edge

If you do make the team, congratulations! But know that your work is just beginning. You now have the responsibility to get better every single practice. Do not take your selection for granted, because chances are, the players who were cut are making plans to get better. If you're not picked for the team, try to understand that players develop at different rates and times. As long as you are still being challenged, you will continue to improve. And most importantly, keep playing and keep having fun! Hockey is a great game.

## 4.1. Hockey Tryouts vs. Job Interview

*By Sharon Enck*

It's that most wonderful time of year: the hockey tryout. It really should be considered a season all its own owing to the preparation, stress, and craziness that comes with it. Long before the dates are announced the speculation starts. Who is leaving? Who is trying out? Is there a new coach? Did you hear that so-and-so is coming from such-and-such?

Nuts, I tell you.

### Just Like a Job Interview

Take it from someone who has been there, it's extremely stressful. Let's follow the process and see just how closely they resemble each other.

### Send in Your Resume

. . . or in this case your player's application for tryouts. While sending in your resume doesn't require a fee, the youth hockey tryout application sure does. A resume and application both show your qualifications by listing where you have worked and where your child has played. And like a job search, your kid usually isn't putting in just one application either.

### Preparation

In the time between turning in your application and the actual interview or tryout, you are preparing. For a job you are researching the company, discovering key players, and looking for news that you can use. For hockey, you're looking at the spring camps, clinics, and private lessons that keep your player at his or her sharpest. Finding out who the coach is and asking around to find out what the team may or may not be looking for are other steps you can take. Like I said, it may as well be another season. Hockey parents in the know call it the "mid-season."

### Dress to Impress

For an interview you need to wear company- and position-appropriate clothing, but what about for hockey? Well, it's not about what you wear, just that you brought it all. Nothing worse than a delay getting on the ice because of a forgotten helmet or pads. Well, nothing worse except for the hockey-mom wrath that your player incurs for you having to drive all the way home to get whatever they forgot!

### Play Nice

It is important to look your interviewer in the eye, give a firm handshake, and thank them for their time. In hockey your player should introduce themselves whenever possible, as well as be polite and respectful of the coaches' time. No horsing around with their buddies or half-assing a drill. This is called putting your best foot, or skate, forward.

### Show Off (In a Good Way)

This is not the time to be modest, shy, or retiring. The wall-flowers are not going to get the job or the spot on the team. In a job interview you need to be ready with solid questions and a knowledge of the organization. In hockey, don't sit on the sidelines. It's the player with initiative who's first for every drill or the goalie who stakes a claim in net before any-one else that is going to get noticed.

### Know Your Competition

Find out who had the job last, his or her strengths and weak-nesses, and why that person left. In hockey you can do the same and find out what the coach is looking for. A defense-man who can score? A goalie who plays the puck? Show off skills like good teamwork if the team has struggled with puck hogs in the past.

### Be a Good Sport

You always want to thank your interviewer with a post-in-terview email or even handwritten card. Your player should thank all the coaches involved and help clear off nets and pucks if the opportunity presents itself. Bonus points for supporting the other players trying out with a fist bump or similar token of hockey appreciation.

### The Aftermath

Got the job? Made the team? Celebrate! But be respectful of those who didn't make it. This can be a tough time and we have all been there. You didn't get the job? Your player didn't make the team? Usually that just means that you weren't the right fit for the company or your player wasn't the right fit for the team. Keep the sour grapes where they belong, in the bottle of wine you will consume before breaking the news to your player. Kidding . . . sort of.

### Keep Moving Forward

There are other jobs and tryouts ahead. Your player needs to keep shooting for the moon, at the very least they will land among the stars.

## 4.2. Ways to Get through a Youth Hockey Tryout

*By Sharon Enck*

Heart is racing, adrenaline is pumping, and you're worried, afraid, and stressed all at the same time. No, you aren't running a marathon; you are at a youth hockey tryout.

Will they be able to keep up? Will they make the team? Will the other three goalies all come down with mono on the critical last day?

Kidding on that last one . . . I think.

Nothing will unravel the coolest hockey mom quicker than a hockey tryout. It's an all-in, high stakes kind of deal. Your player has identified which team they want to play for, you've paid your tryout fees, marked those days with big red circles on your calendar, and now it's go time.

I would guess that the moms and dads sitting on the bleachers, standing behind the glass or in the warm room feel way more anxiety than the most nervous of player.

And why wouldn't we? We want our player to be successful, to be happy, to beat out that really big goalie that came out of nowhere with a great glove . . . oops, sorry.

So, how do you get through the process without succumbing to the tension and nerves? Here are some tips that I swear by:

1. Don't watch your player too closely. There's nothing worse than having your nose pressed up on the glass, analyzing every move, and seeing every "mistake" up close and personal. And yes, that goes for you too goalie parents!

2. Use the "hear-no-evil, speak-no-evil, see-no-evil" method of hockey parenting. Don't judge the other players, parents, or coaches, or that really big goalie who just came out of nowhere. Negativity breeds stress and you are under a lot already . . . those hockey bills are enough.

3. Resist the urge to speak to the coach at tryouts. He or she doesn't have the time to get into an involved

discussion with you right then . . . during tryouts . . . with a hundred other parents listening in. Not the time.

4. Try to keep your player's emotions in check. They aren't "stupid" and they are not "the worst player out there." Even if they didn't perform all that well. Again, negativity breeds stress. They don't need it either.

5. Use discretion when celebrating and don't be the sour grapes parent if you aren't able do the celebrating yourself. Sometimes we just don't know what coaches are looking for in a player, what they need to round out the team, or the type of skills or effort they are scouting. Be happy for your newly rostered player but be respectful of those who didn't make the cut. And if you are on the cutting room floor? Don't throw shade (it's really fun using a fourteen-year-old's vernacular) at the organization, coaches, other parents, or players. I have known several parents who have been blacklisted from a rink or association because of a badly worded email, phone call, or tantrums thrown in the lobby.

6. Have some wine. No, really. I have several hockey mom friends who have a glass or two at the rink bar in anticipation of their nerves. Who are we to judge? If it's not broken, don't fix it.

As for me, I clench my teeth, wring my hands, and try to talk about other things. And I never press my nose against the glass . . . even when a really big goalie comes out of nowhere!

Good luck and let me know how you handle the stress of tryouts!

# 5

# PRESEASON MEETING PUTS EVERYONE ON THE SAME PAGE

**E**verybody knows there is no crying in baseball. Legendary football coach John Heisman used to preach, "Gentleman, it is better to have died a small boy than to fumble this football." And of course, Herb Brooks famously proclaimed that great moments are born from great opportunity.

Despite what those "Coaching for Dummies" books might have you believe, there really is no one-size-fits-all philosophy for coaching. Every coach is different.

A preseason meeting can be a great opportunity to find out if a coach's particular philosophy fits with what your family is looking for during the season.

Minnesota hockey mom Lisa Mackeben, who assists with the Champlin Park Youth Hockey Association, says practice attendance, communication, financial issues, and safety top her list of items she wants addressed during the preseason meeting.

"I remember this meeting being very important the first season my son, Jack, played hockey," Lisa said. "I like and expect coaches to speak to their expectations for the season, so we're all on the same page."

Concord, Massachusetts, hockey parents Jessica and Steve Kennedy say a coach's attitude can be everything when it comes to developing skills and a love for the game.

"A youth hockey coach should foster a fun and encouraging atmosphere, especially for impressionable younger players," Steve said. "It could be hard to determine the coach's attitude during the first meeting, so a bit of 'research' talking to other families can go a long way toward finding out what you are getting yourself into."

It helps when coaches set clear boundaries as to when they're willing to talk to parents. Our coach let us know up front about the "twenty-four-hour rule" after a game before talking to him. That cooling off period can help you put things in perspective.

This is also the time to figure out your hockey budget. What will the season cost, and how many fundraisers can you realistically pull off? Decide, as a team, how far and how often everyone is willing to travel. Find out about parent involvement, too.

While it's not likely that Scotty Bowman is coaching your Jim Craig-in-training, it's still important for you as a parent to understand how the coach approaches the game. You want to know that he or she will look out for your child's safety and wellbeing, but also help maximize and develop his or her on-ice talents.

Don't be that parent. "Hockey Yeller" *Credit:* Darren Gygi

# 6

# SETTING GOALS FOR THE SEASON: FOR YOUR PLAYER AND YOURSELF

---

**There's a classic** line muttered by the titular character in *Ferris Bueller's Day Off*: "Life moves pretty fast. If you don't stop and look around once in a while, you could miss it."

Ferris's words don't just apply to playing hooky from school; they also apply to playing the role of hockey mom or dad. With all the time, money, and energy (and then more time, money, and energy) we pour into our little ones' on-ice careers, it's easy to slip into the same old routine.

What I love about a new season is that it's like a freshly resurfaced sheet of ice. We get the chance to erase bumps and rough patches, and break away from past mistakes.

For Syracuse hockey parents Cathe and Dan Babbage, annual season objectives include building relationships and putting their kids in a position where they are competing at their highest levels. With nineteen seasons devoted to their two kids, the Babbages have had plenty of time to perfect their list.

"We expect the kids to work hard in every situation and always be good teammates," Cathe says.

And while their children play at different levels, the same simple philosophy applies to both.

"We've always made sure to communicate with the kids about what's important," she says. "Making sure that we are listening to them and hearing what their goals are, not making assumptions based on what others are doing."

My fellow Syracuse Nationals hockey mom Angela Palmer contends that goals aren't just set on the ice. "It was important for me to teach my daughter at a young age the meaning of a true athlete," says Palmer. "I always want her to make good choices in regards to friends, social settings, and high-pressure scenarios. Hockey means so much to her. She knows that it's not an expectation or a given that she'll play. Her behavior off the ice is just as important as it is during games," says Palmer.

Listening to our kids is key, and so is watching them. Really watching them. This will be the season Phoenix, Arizona, goalie mom Sharon Enck tunes in to the moment.

"My goal is to look up often, despite managing the team's social media," she says. "Even though I do it for a living and want to help the team, there will be no live tweeting or periscoping during games. It's too frustrating to be worried about posts loading and missing important moments, like an amazing save."

I've also noticed more than a few moms and dads in the stands looking up between text messages and social media feeds—swiping, scrolling, or reading while son or daughter is passing, scoring, and making saves. Do you notice your smartphone's ping before a ref's whistle? Don't think your kids don't notice. #HockeyParentFail.

So this season, put down the cell phones, tear your eyes away from the tablet, and live in the moment.

After all, hockey—like our children's youth careers—moves pretty fast. If we don't stop and look around once in a while, we could miss it.

Joe, Christie and Sophia Burns make the yearly pledge to keep hockey fun.
*Credit:* Jim Lamanna

# 7

# A PARENT'S PLEDGE TO MAKE THIS SEASON SPECIAL

**The Greek playwright** Sophocles lived some 2,500 years ago, so it's a good bet he wasn't a hockey dad. Still, even though he may never have spent the weekend huddled under a blanket in a frigid rink, the wordsmith was onto something when he noted, "The keenest sorrow is to recognize ourselves as the sole cause of all our adversities."

As hockey parents, we know exactly what those "adversities" are—vilifying refs, loudly lamenting your child's ice time, and using language more colorful than a Matisse canvas. Luckily, each new season affords us the opportunity to make amends and begin anew.

So let's take that first step, by joining others in a pledge to be a better hockey parent this season, by promising to do the following:

- I pledge to give my kids plenty of time to get their gear on. I will not rush them! —*Alyse Cullen, Moorehead, Minnesota*

- To always remember our children's coach volunteers his or her time and to always keep that in mind before saying anything. —*Stephanie and Matt MacDerment, Syracuse, New York*
- No more car coaching after a game. —*Steve Kellogg, Baldwinsville, New York*
- To bond more with families and parents on the team. —*Angela Palmer, Baldwinsville, New York*
- I pledge to focus on skill development rather than wins and losses. —*Kevin Bernard, Manchester, New York*
- To be more involved and do more for the team. —*Anna Sharpe, New Hartford, New York*
- Be careful with "constructive criticism" after a game. Trust that my child tried hard and did the best he or she could. —*Jessica and Steve Kennedy, Concord, Massachusetts*
- Savor every moment and try not to cry when my son plays his last year of hockey. —*Cindy Weller McHarris, Sauquoit, New York*
- Embrace my daughter's goalie eccentricities and position reputation of being just a little left of center. —*Sharon Enck, Phoenix, Arizona*
- Bring more snacks, take more pictures, cheer louder, and smile more. —*Melissa Alcott, Rochester, New York*
- Try not to jump out of my seat every time he takes a hit in his first season as a Bantam. —*Stacy Schavnis Doherty, Honey Brook, Pennsylvania*
- Keep my mouth shut. —*Charlie Hamilton, Washington, DC*
- Stay positive in my cheering and try not to roll my eyes at the parents who have no clue about the game. Keep

my mama bear instinct hidden deep down when people are yelling at my son. —*Monica Hudak Headley, Mead, Washington*

- I promise to listen to my kids after a game, before I share my opinions. —*Effi Christou, Skaneateles, New York*
- Bring more Snickers bars for the out-of-control parents. —*Robin Johnson Virgilio, Lincolnwood, Illinois*
- Set reasonable goals for my players and celebrate like crazy when they achieve them. —*Mike Braciszewski, Syracuse, New York*
- Try not to beat myself up when I can't go to my daughter's tournament in Ottawa because my son has a tournament in Connecticut. —*Tamatha Picolla, New Hartford, New York*
- To watch calmly like an adult and the role model that I am. —*Daniel Edison, Chicago Illinois*
- Stand back a little more and let my son grow into the great player and person I know he has the potential to be. —*Heather Delaney Doran, Fulton, New York*
- Not to let other people's ignorance bother me or my son's play. —*Laura Bell, Smithtown, New York*
- Ask my son to dry his own equipment. —*Amy Moon, Syracuse, New York*
- Do more team-building activities. —*Alison Spears, Ogdensburg, New.York.*
- Promote a positive learning environment, even when there are disappointments. —*Julie Varney, Baldwinsville, New York*
- Be my child's biggest cheerleader, not his biggest critic. —*Tammy Myers, Auburn, New York*

- Enjoy my son's last year at home before hockey takes him away. —*Pam Munson, Baldwinsville, New York*
- Enjoy the early morning games and the late night practices because I am present, in the moment, watching my children loving their sport and these moments are priceless! —*Becki Sporre, Syracuse, New York*
- Stockpile toe warmers. —*Tom Groat Stock, Unadilla, New York*
- Don't initiate a critique of the game and your child unless he or she asks you, even though you are chomping at the bit. —*Fred Cowett, Ithaca, New York*
- And as for me, even with the added pressure of my daughter playing AAA Tier 1 hockey, I promise to always remember the cardinal kids' sports rule: "Keep it fun." After all, anything short of that would be a tragedy of Greek proportions.

Preparation is key to winning the battle each season. *Credit:* Darren Gygi.

# 8

## GETTING READY TO GO TEN ROUNDS THIS SEASON

**A**sk any prizefighter—or even a good hockey player— and he or she will tell you: the fight is won not in the ring, but in the preparation beforehand.

So while it is incumbent upon your young skater to practice and prepare for success, we parents can set a good example by following a few simple steps:

### Equipment Check

Check the gear from head to toe and every neutral zone in between. Chances are your hockey player grew a little during the offseason (both of mine did, a lot) and may not fit into some (or all) of their gear. While we're all looking to save a buck, this isn't the place to skimp. It's not just a matter of comfort, but of safety as well.

Not sure if you can get another year out of the gear? Auburn, New York, hockey mom Jackie Reilly has the experts at her local retail hockey store judge what's good and what may need to be replaced. She also picks up spare blades, laces, mouth guards, and tape.

Then it's off to the drug store to stock up on ibuprofen and disinfectant wipes. It all gets packed in a travel crate stored in her Suburban—along with hoodies, blankets, gloves, spare shirts, books, and odor ban travel spray.

## Control Your Corner

As big or bad as any fighter may be, a prizefighter is only as good as his or her trainer. As the person in charge of the corner, make sure your player knows the rules of the game, on and off the ice. School comes first, and a solid sleep schedule is vital. Family time, rest, and relaxation need to be in your lives, too.

## The Weigh In

The preseason team meeting can be one of the most important events of the season. It will help you determine costs, travel plans, goals for the team, the coach's philosophy, and give you a chance to develop a good relationship with the coach.

## Gut Check

Phoenix, Arizona, hockey mom Sharon Enck has a heart-to-heart with her goalie daughter before the start of each season, asking what she's excited and nervous about and what she wants to work on. "Of course, I don't interrogate her all at once because she would probably just clam up if I did," Enck says. "I drop these questions in during a car ride or on a walk to get the 'real' answers."

She also does the nose a favor with a good old fashioned sterilization of smelly equipment. The motto for her entourage? "Begin fresh and end filthy."

## Answering the Final Bell

Put in the time before you get ready to rumble, and you and yours can stay off the canvas this season and skate away with the championship belt.

# 9

# A WORD TO THE WISE:
# CHOOSE YOUR WORDS WISELY

In **January of** 2016, Joel Quenneville became the second-winningest coach in NHL history. Only Scotty Bowman has stood behind the bench and won more hockey games.

These two coaching icons have won so many times that they make it look easy. But as the proverb goes, every journey of a thousand miles begins with a single step. Even the most established coach had to start somewhere, learning valuable lessons along the way.

Sometimes we as parents don't take the time to walk a mile in our coaches' shoes. We can forget that they are people too—with lives outside of the rink. We sometimes forget that they are giving of themselves to coach our sons and daughters, to impart life lessons that will last long after our kids leave the rink. Sometimes we also forget that they are human beings.

We need to remember those things the next time we get frustrated with our child's ice time, or how a game or even a season shakes out. Sometimes we just need to let a little time pass to reflect on a situation and try to see it from another perspective.

When challenging a coach, Cicero, New York, hockey dad Pete Ludden uses the twenty-four-hour rule. If something happens during a game that he thinks needs to be addressed, he'll wait at least until the next day before bringing it up.

"It allows the individuals to be a little removed from the situation in case there are emotions attached to the subject to be discussed," he says. "It also gives the person time to think about what they want to say, how they want to say it, and if it's necessary to say it at all."

We all love our kids and will do anything in our power to protect them from what we see as life's injustices. If you feel the coach isn't exactly in tune with how all his or her players are feeling, consider some diplomacy when it comes time to speak up.

Sometimes, it may be better to empower your child to take the lead. That's what Monica Headley did when her son felt that he was getting cheated out of playing time. This hockey mom from Mead, Washington, encouraged him to speak up for himself.

"My son, who is always voted the captain or alternate, is a kid who doesn't talk much. He worked up the nerve to talk to the head coach about not being on penalty kills," Headley says.

It turns out the coach didn't have a reason and apologized for the oversight. Headley says her son felt empowered because he took matters into his own hands when it came to his ice time.

It's also important to consider that any interaction you have with the coach, no matter how well meaning, could potentially impact your child. After all, no child wants to have the reputation on the team as having one *those* parents.

So the next time parental instincts tell you to call out the coach, make sure it's the right call. As Quenneville says, "You get rewarded when you do a lot of things right."

# 10

## CARS ARE FOR TRANSPORTATION, NOT COACHING

### By Mark Gilman

**Yes, I'm old** enough to remember the television classic, *Leave It to Beaver*. For those who have never seen the show, there were constant discussions of whether Ward Cleaver, the dad and disciplinarian, was being too hard on his son, Beaver. Of course he wasn't, but it was a running commentary throughout most episodes. In the same vein, I've been around a lot of hockey parents over the years who wonder if the coaches are being too hard on our kids. I don't know about you, but the coaches my kids have played for tend to be far kinder to them than their own parents.

I've lectured to parents for years about "car coaching." This is the act of playing coach all the way home from a game where we do all we can to suck the fun out of every game, no matter what age they are. One of the reasons I write about it is to remind myself to stop doing it. It's really hard. You have things in your head that, for whatever reason, you feel necessary to "get out" before the poor kid gets home. The longer the drive, the more dreadful the experience. This is one thing I always remind myself of: that when your kid is on the ice, you're watching every move they make. Every shift. You're following them around the ice, you see every nuance. Let me tell you something, no one on the bench or the stands watches your kid that much and no kid deserves that kind of scrutiny. We all do it and we all need to knock it off and relax. After one particular game, my son's mother said, "I thought he played a really good game today." My response? "Seriously? He didn't backcheck, he was on the wrong wing half the time, he . . ." She responded with, "I'll take him home." Point made. I never forgot it.

This brings me back to coaches. I actually like it when coaches jump on my kid, because it's usually for a reason. Could be they are trying to motivate him, maybe they're trying to instill in him some discipline, maybe (probably) he just completely ignored everything the coach just told him. Whatever the reason, it's usually a good thing. I've told my kids, no matter the sport, that if your coaches never say anything to you, that's a bad sign. It means they don't care. It means they don't see you as a priority. It may also mean that he or she has written you off.

Which brings me back to parents. Maybe, just maybe, you had a bad day and taking it out on your kid on the way home is your way of venting? Maybe your kid isn't as skilled as you'd like but it's who they are? It's not his or her fault. Yelling at kids (especially under the age of fifteen) for the way they play during the game is the worst thing a hockey parent can do to their kids. We've all done it and we all regret it (hopefully). Kids under fifteen haven't finished developing or they're in the middle of it, or they're confused, or they're tired from school, or their girlfriend just broke up with them. Sometimes that's all it takes. How about we just lay off the kids and go back to observing the twenty-four-hour rule before we "coach" them. The next time you think your kid's coach is being "too hard on Beaver," you might want to do an assessment of your own conversations with the same kid this year.

# 11

## WHERE'S THE HOCKEY MOMS' GREEN JACKET OR HARD HAT?

### By Sharon Enck

**A green jacket is** the pinnacle of success on my daughter's hockey team. It holds the prestige of being rewarded to the hardest working player on the ice during a particular game. It gets passed from player to player depending who has earned it that game. The proud recipient gets to wear it until the next game; the next victor has been decided by the coach.

Many teams have their own version of the green jacket; the most popular that I've seen is the hard hat. And, in my experience, the kids take it seriously. It's a badge of honor that gives that player some bragging right, at least until the next game, knowing that coach picked them as the "it" player.

So, here's the real question . . . where is the hard hat or the green jacket for the hardest working hockey mom (or dad)? Where's our badge of honor? Our swag?

I came up with a list of reasons a hard hat or green jacket should be awarded to the hardest working parent on the team.

1. They don't talk garbage about the team, the coach, or other parents.
2. They cheer at games, don't pick fights with opposing parents, and refrain from yelling instructions at their player on the ice.
3. They don't shirk their locker room parent duties.
4. Their ride home speech consists only of, "Great job, did you have fun?"
5. They have an extra of everything in their kid's hockey bag.

Yes, that list is for the already perfect parents, the ones we all aspire to be. For the rest of us it goes like this:

1. Managed to get your player to the rink, on time with all of their gear for all the week's practices.
2. Didn't weep or throw themselves on the ground in a temper tantrum when yet another out-of-state trip was scheduled.
3. Was able to correctly identify the rink where the game was held that week, before heading to the wrong one first.
4. Politely held our tongue and only glared when an opposing parent referred to your goalie as "lucky."
5. Despite all the challenges, still loves youth hockey.

So, I ask, where is it? Because green is definitely my color.

# 12

## WHAT TO EXPECT FROM YOUR EXPECTATIONS

"You play . . . to win the game! Hello!"

Those are the words of Herm Edwards, former NFL player turned head coach, who may be best remembered for his post-game summation on the reason one plays a particular sport.

Edward's philosophy may work for hulking millionaires who play on national TV, but for the younger generation who try to emulate them, it's important to temper those expectations. Sports can't simply be seen as tool for material gain.

When my husband and I recently delivered our son to Bentley University in Boston sans hockey bag, some friends and family were shocked.

"What? He's not playing hockey in college? After all these years?"

That kind of reaction doesn't surprise Plymouth, Michigan, hockey mom Laurie Golden, creator of *The Trophy Mom* blog. Countless times, she has seen parents make the mistake of concentrating all efforts on one sport, with extra coaching thinking it will pay off with a scholarship.

"My husband and I joke that if people took all the money they spent on camps, special training, and extra coaching and invested it, they'd have no problem paying for college," Golden says.

While playing hockey in college was never on our son's radar, or ours frankly, early on in his life it was clear that hockey was his passion.

Kellie Merrill from Wasilla, Alaska, saw that same kind of natural passion in her peewee-aged daughter.

"She loves hockey twenty-four/seven as much as my husband and I do."

But her son? Not so much. The lack of enthusiasm led to a heart to heart before his bantam year, which resulted in a switch from the rink to the pool.

"As a parent I am passionate about watching my children enjoy what they are doing instead of seeing a lackluster performance because they think that is what I expect them to be doing," Merrill says.

Parents not only need to set realistic expectations for their children, they also need to set them for themselves.

"It's really easy to lose your perspective," says Golden, whose oldest son played as a senior baseball player for Eastern Michigan University, while another son played in the American Collegiate Hockey Association ACHA for Oakland University, and a daughter who who did a lot of traveling while playing for the 19U Michigan Icebreakers Tier One girls hockey league.

"You have to make a conscious decision to stay focused on what's best for your child and your family. Now that my kids are older, each of them has thanked us for being sane, level-headed sports parents. The kids really are watching."

Playing hockey was great for our son, who gained confidence, friends, and leadership skills.

So in the end, I guess Coach Edwards was right—you do play to win the game. Just not the one on the ice, but the game of life.

Sometimes we forget to act like adults. *Credit:* Darren Gygi

# 13

## OH BEHAVE! HOW TO ACT LIKE AN ADULT AT A YOUTH HOCKEY GAME

**We hockey parents** are a fiery, passionate group who often wear our hearts on our sleeves. It's when our tongues get ahead of us in the stands that it can get bad and downright ugly. When hockey parents act like children, nobody wins.

Here are a few suggestions to help parents act like adults at a youth hockey game.

### Don't Be That Parent

"Hit him!" "Puck hog!" You better skate if you want a ride home!" "Forget your glasses, ref?" Any of this sound familiar?

It's a good thing our kids are wearing helmets with ear guards to help drown out the critical cries from moms and dads in the stands. Yelling at your kid isn't going to make him or her skate any faster or shoot any better. Having a meltdown over missed penalties or screaming at the referees won't score you any more points either.

It will help you lose respect among your fellow parents, and if you're loud and nasty enough, it might earn you a ticket to the parking lot.

## Set a Good Example

It's not always easy, but parents need to chill in the stands. Your kids watch and learn from you.

There are a number of ways you set examples of good adult behavior, all while sitting in the stands. Let's say the other team is really struggling. While you may be thrilled with the remarkable lead of your team, imagine what it feels like for the other team and their parents. So temper your enthusiasm after the sixth goal and subdue those cheers and claps. Keep it classy.

## Easy to Make, Easy to Break

Go back to that code of conduct you signed at the beginning of the season. Are you playing by the rules and being hyper supportive or being hyper critical? Or maybe just plain hyper. Are you biting your tongue when you see players on your team miss a pass or fail to take that seemingly easy shot? Let's take a moment and make some promises we will do our best to keep:

1. Make a promise to yourself not to say a single critical word about the officials during and after a game.
2. Tell your child what they did right and let the coach tell them what went wrong.

How can we teach our kids to love a game when all they see and hear from the stands is negativity and hate?

# 14

## KEEP YOUR FOCUS HOCKEY PARENTS

**N**ancy Duffy was a television newswoman when men dominated the industry. And she was also someone who never let a challenge stand in her way: a black belt in karate, a woman in government service, and a single mom raising two active boys. She was amazing. And she was the first hockey mom I ever knew.

She shattered the glass ceiling time and time again, paving the way for working women who followed. She was my hero both professionally and at home. And she had the right words for any situation.

Whenever I feel myself drawn in by the craziness, the gossip, and the tension that crops up during a long hockey season, I turn to an article Nancy wrote many years ago . . . after the National Sports Festival of 1981. It reminds me that it's not the trophies or win/loss count that really matter. It's the time you spend with your kid, and the fact that you're not just raising someone good at sports, but a good sport, too.

For me, it puts everything in perspective.

## A Hockey Mom Fights Back

*By Nancy Duffy*

After a year and a half, I'm still smarting from the prejudice I endured as a newswoman trying to cover the National Sports Festival's hockey tournament. I had crashed the all-male news conference of Bobby Carpenter, then the top high school hockey player in the nation and now a Washington Capitol. Glares seared me like the red light behind a goalie having a bad night. I could almost hear my fellow reporters say, "What does she know about hockey?"

The situation was frustrating for me as a reporter. For myself as a hockey mom, having lived in locker rooms for eight years, it was laughable.

So now, in the name of mothers everywhere who have ever laced up a skate at ten below, it's time to set the record straight. Hockey moms live the game as intensely as any fan and assuredly more so than any sports reporter, judging by my encounters in sports departments.

The hockey mom is truly a model of unacclaimed virtue, a paragon of womanhood tested beyond all limits. She is someone who shivers at 4,015 rink sides from Elmira to Ottawa, from Niagara to New Jersey, and who drives through four-hour blizzards for a one-hour game. She buys a hundred-dollar ice skates instead of furniture, lives six months in long underwear with skate guards in her pockets, and carries maps of Montreal in her purse.

I dare say no sports reporter has ever gotten his slant on the sport by sifting through the moldy mysteries of a hockey bag, tripping over hockey pucks in drape folds, or trying to maneuver past hundreds of splintered hockey sticks, too good to be thrown out, in the upstairs closet. That's not to mention the 5:00 a.m. practices, the noon games, and the 6:00 p.m. scrimmages—all on the same day, in three different towns. Sports reporters have never dealt with other kids' fathers who are coaches and referees or struggled with the staunch maternal-ism of other hockey moms. They don't really know the sting of defeat or the agony of the bench that only a mom can feel.

"What does she know about hockey?" sports reporters ask. "What do they know?" I reply. Do they know the trick of matching unmatched hockey socks? Have sports guys ever figured out how to rig a one-size-fits-all hockey garter on a five-year-old body or how to keep the slats from sliding out of the hems of hockey pants, or the secret of unraveling hockey tape?

Even if they knew these secrets, would they have the patience to spend their free time squeezing growing feet into last month's new skates or be willing to finance thousands of trips to the skate sharpener? I think not.

But a hockey mom does it year after year. She lugs the hockey bags on her shoulders when her child is a tyke, bakes cookies for the locker room when he's a squirt, and billets young Canadian teenagers when he's a bantam. A hockey mom is committed from the time her wobbly legged four-year-old pushes a chair while on the ice for balance at 5:00 a.m. practice.

There are no holidays or timeouts for a hockey mom. The day after Christmas is always spent on the road to a tournament. It's almost Easter before the season ends. That means six months of car breakdowns in Massena, whiteouts in Pulaski, and enough trips across the International Bridge to earn Canadian citizenship. Hockey moms don't flinch when they hear that five more games have been added to the schedule, though. They just postpone their cleaning and cooking for one more month.

There are tribes in New Zealand that inflict pain on their victims in more subtle ways than the game of hockey on moms. But the hockey mom endures and pays the price as long as the ice is available. Somehow the twelve- and thirteen-year-olds who cuddle their hockey sticks in the night make it all worthwhile.

So come on you sports guys. Give us hockey moms a break.

# 15

## TWENTY-FOUR-HOUR RULE HELPS COOLER HEADS PREVAIL

**I bet there** are times when coaches wish they could unleash a pocket-sized Zamboni after a game. This machine would smooth over tension, anger, and frustration of "stop watch" parents the same way the real Zamboni turns rough ice smooth again.

There's no magical way to avoid some conflicts, but something called the Twenty-Four-Hour Rule has been a great help.

It works like this: wait twenty-four hours before talking to a coach or a parent after a game about something that troubled you during the game.

Thomas Winn, a hockey dad from Camillus, New York, calls it the "Golden Rule" for hockey parents. "It allows us to take a step back, think about all sides of the issue and then, without being in the heat of the moment, approach the coach with your concerns," Winn says.

It also gives a coach the opportunity to assess the situation and discuss issues fairly once emotions are not as raw as an exposed nerve.

Oswego, New York, Minor Hockey Association President Dan Bartlett says it's hard to tell how many conflicts have been avoided because cooler heads have prevailed because of the rule. "I have been told countless stories of upset parents ready to blow their tops, but they followed the rule and in the process never even mentioned the issue to a coach," he says.

The twenty-year veteran coach says he has used the rule with his teams for as long as he can remember, and that most, if not all of the confrontations with parents occurred when the twenty-four-hour rule wasn't followed.

New Jersey hockey-playing dad Brent Dolan, writer at uppercornerhockey.com, is also a big fan of the rule.

"Sports can bring out the energy and passion in people," he says. "I don't think they mean any harm, but when something happens they think is unfair, they'll voice their opinions right then and there."

Dolan says the twenty-four-hour rule, combined with a zero tolerance policy, can help players enjoy and focus more on the game and not be subjected to ugly locker room or lobby scenes afterward.

Noelle DeSantis, a hockey mom, says we owe it to our kids to show them how better decisions are made when you are calm.

"During the game, emotions are running high and we tend to use our reptilian brain—fight or flight," she says. "But when it comes to making actual decisions that impact people, we need to use our cortex [higher level thinking]."

So the next time you're about to get into the face of your coach, bite your tongue and unleash that emotional Zamboni in your mind. The next day, I bet you'll feel as smooth and cool as that freshly resurfaced sheet of ice.

# 16

## DEALING WITH MR. AND MRS. KNOW-IT-ALL

*"I am not young enough to know everything."*
—Oscar Wilde

You would think the older we get, the wiser we would become. Unfortunately, the opposite seems to be true, especially when it comes to youth sports.

Being a hockey parent comes with more than just smelly pads and lost sleep. It also means dealing with all kinds of parents, among them Mr. and Mrs. Know-It-All.

The Know-It-Alls seem to have missed their true calling as hockey coaches. Even without the same background and experience as Brooks, Bowman, and Babcock, in their minds they have all the answers when it comes to power-play units and line combinations. And most of the time they are not shy about sharing their opinions from their perch in the bleachers or while milling about the lobby after the game.

The problems grow when the Know-It-Alls decide to share all their wisdom with the coach, which can sour a season very quickly.

As Mark Gilman explains, "They think they know more than the coach. This is an infection waiting to strike your team chemistry, and it has to be disinfected early before it spreads."

Once a parent has a coach's ear, look out, cautions Syracuse University Women's Hockey Coach Paul Flanagan. "The next step is that parent is perceived as making decisions for the team, and that can be an ugly scenario," Flanagan says.

When that happens, Flanagan makes it a practice of thanking the parent for their insight, then asks what time he should be ready to catch a ride to work with them, so he can assist with them with their job.

Both Gilman and Flanagan encourage coaches to engage parents before the season starts and set some parameters. "Let them know you are the coach, and while not perfect, you will be running the team exclusively this year," Gilman says.

Cicero-North Syracuse, New York, hockey mom Chrissie Sarosy deals with the Know-It-Alls by strategically staking a place far away from the "experts," and sitting near parents who simply want to enjoy the game.

Jodi Lind-Anderson prefers to give the Know-It-Alls something to chew on—literally. The author of *Hockey Moms Aren't Crazy* once delivered a well-relished hot dog to a very loud goalie dad who felt compelled to vociferously express his dissatisfaction with the team's defense. Upon handing over the hot dog, Anderson reminded Mr. Know-It-All that his goaltending daughter was part of the defense.

After all, most Know-It-Alls still have a thing or two to learn.

# 17

## A LACK OF ICE TIME CAN MAKE A PARENT'S BLOOD BOIL

**There are two** words that can leave a hockey parent feeling merry or miserable over the course of a hockey season. Those two words are "ice time."

Let's face it, nothing will make a parent's blood boil quicker than watching their son or daughter parked on the end of the bench like an old car sitting on cinderblocks in the driveway.

Who can blame them? Every parent wants their child to get as much ice time as any other kid, and at the youth level they should.

As John Walsh, an assistant coach with the Syracuse Stars program, has seen, sometimes coaches forget their role and what youth hockey participation is really all about.

"Most young coaches put pressure on themselves to win. I was like that when I first started," says Walsh, who has been coaching for close to four decades. "In time I learned that even though I hate to lose, my main role is to make players better."

Making players better means giving them a chance to play in both practices and games.

At the younger levels, Walsh says all players should play a regular shift in every game. Coaches always have the option of putting a weaker player on a line with two stronger players, and giving top lines a little more ice time when the game is on the line.

East Carolina Hockey Association mom Kimberly Smith Lukhard says jumping into the travel hockey arena meant her family has had to develop thick skin, since the coach would not guarantee her son would play. Her boys needed to understand making practices and giving 100 percent was the price to pay for ice time.

"I would only speak to the coach about our sons getting short changed if I saw it happening shift after shift, game after game," she says.

As the author of *Eat, Skate, Win,* Smith Lukhard feels that hockey teaches her children valuable life lessons that will stick with them long after they've left the rink. Those lessons can also apply to mom and dad. "As parents we learn one of the most valuable lessons," she says. "We can't make it happen for our children on the ice. It's up to them."

Still, as George Gwozdecky, former University of Denver coach, says, there should only be a few reasons for youth hockey coaches to shorten their bench. Those reasons should be for issues such as sickness, injuries, or breaking team rules.

"Shortening the bench in order to win a youth hockey game is absurd," says Gwozdecky, who won two national titles while at DU. "The job of a coach is to develop every player's physical skills within the team's parameters while at the same time teaching the important skills of discipline, team-first attitude, tenacity, sacrifice, and work ethic."

Playing a short bench, while usually done to improve a team's chances of winning, can have the opposite effect. Not only will some players get discouraged, but the fact that the team is not developing any level of quality depth could come back to bite a coach as the season winds down.

Through trial and error, John Walsh has learned that victory is sweet, but developing skaters into better players and people is an even sweeter reward.

# 18

## YOU DON'T HAVE TO BE THAT HOCKEY PARENT

---

**W**e've all met them before (and if you haven't met them, then we're probably talking about you): The Despicable Hockey Parent. They're the ones hurling insults during a heated game, berating refs, or acting like Scotty Bowman from the stands.

Before you fall into this trap, why not consider the following, and make a run for The Respectable Parent?

### Honor

Learn the value of restraint. It's something Arizona goalie mom Sharon Enck has tried to achieve. "Everyone will forgive you if you forget the team snack, but may not be as quick to turn the other cheek if you spew obscenities at a game," she says.

Enck says it's best to avoid being the parent everyone hates, for your sake and your child's.

And for the game's sake, parent behavior needs to change, says Kevyn Adams, the vice president and director at the Academy of Hockey, HarborCenter in Buffalo, New York.

"It seems that in sports today, the concept of good sportsmanship is lost and parents should remember to behave in an honorable way that we would want our kids to emulate in the future," he says.

## Active (But Not Over-Reactive)

After years of playing, coaching, and going to rinks with his own son, Adams has yet to come across a kid who likes losing. But a loss can be a win, with the right spin.

"Leave it on the ice," says Adams, who played eleven years in the NHL. "Encourage them to control the factors that they have control over, such as giving 100 percent effort on the ice."

If you lighten up, Adams says, your kids will enjoy the game more and worry less about the outcome, something which is out of their control.

There's no postgame analysis for Enck.

"I let my daughter talk, uninterrupted, for five minutes after a game," she says. "Once the five minutes are up, we're done."

## Passion

Keep the passion positive and let other mamas have the drama.

"Talking smack about other kids and parents is bad form," Enck says. "And it's a small world, so remember that if your kid stays in the sport long enough you will see them again."

## Patience

Perhaps there's nothing more discouraging to a child than postgame antics by parents.

"In those cases where you do become upset, remove yourself from the environment so your child doesn't see your negativity," Adams says.

## Youth Sports

Sports can bring out the best in us. It can also bring out the worst. Leave "despicable parent" at home. Be that honorable, active, passionate, patient-with-our-youth parent. You'll soon learn that you don't need to be wearing Pharrell's oversized hat to be happy.

Goalies face extra challenges. *Credit:* Darren Gygi

# 19

## GOALIE PARENTS FACE THEIR OWN CHALLENGES WHEN THEIR KIDS STRAP ON THE PADS

**Jacques Plante—one** of the greatest goalies to ever play the position—aptly described the pressure of playing between the pipes as, "How would you like a job where every time you make a mistake, a big red light goes on, and eighteen thousand people boo?"

His take on the position flies right in the face of the famous maxim of Heywood Broun—one of America's first sportswriters—who noted, "Sports do not build character, they reveal it."

But that's what made Plante one of the best backstops in hockey history: a willingness to shoulder not only the heavy pads, but also the pressures of an entire team and its rabid fans.

As a goaltender, you're a part of the team, but you're also an island unto yourself. Your shortcomings are immediately apparent and the finger pointing often starts with you.

So when your Baby Brodeur says he or she wants a blocker and leg pads for Christmas, don't leave them alone on an island.

While it's not easy to watch the rubber fly on the games when they're looking like Swiss cheese, if you can get past the understandable trepidation, you may learn something very special about your child.

"Chances are if your child has chosen to become a goalie, they are much stronger than you think," says veteran hockey mom Diane Pelton of Syracuse.

Being a goalie parent isn't easy either. They're usually the ones standing behind the glass, walking from end to end and yelling, "Cover it" at the top of their lungs. Early on, Pelton heeded the advice from a favorite goalie coach: it's better to be seen and not heard.

"If your goalie is looking at you, they're not focused on the play in front of them," she says.

Stephen Bowker's son knew the moment he strapped on the pads, he wanted to be a goalie. With his son now playing for his JV team, the Wilmington, Massachusetts, dad has learned that kids need to be treated as kids and not pushed too hard.

"It can be nerve-racking at times. They are going to have good and bad games. You have to be supportive," Bowker says.

"It's very hard to watch him get down on himself and go through the emotions of losing a game," adds Auburn, New York, goalie mom Denise Farrington.

"Make sure they know that winning or losing a game does not define them."

When there are more lows than highs, Farrington suggests that it may be time to stack the pads on a shelf in the garage.

It takes a unique temperament to bear the burden between the pipes. But with the right support and nurturing, you may find goaltending reveals something we all want for our kids—that they are special.

## The Seven Stages of Goalie Mom Grief

*By Sharon Enck*

I was thinking about funerals the other day, which is not that odd considering I now pass a boneyard every day coming home, when I got to thinking about grief. It not only applies to friends and family of dearly departed, it also applies to goalie mom grief.

Do the seven stages apply? I think they do. Does any of this sound familiar?

1. Shock: Did that puck just go through the five hole?
2. Denial: No, that couldn't have! Her stick was down, wasn't it?
3. Pain and Guilt: Oh no, the parents are looking at me. Maybe I should have sprung for that extra goalie coaching in addition to the four times a week she is already on the ice.
4. Anger: She KNOWS BETTER!
5. Depression, Reflection, and Loneliness: That puts us down two goals in the third period, what are we going to do? Maybe if she saves everything else and the team steps up offensively, we can pull it out. I better not talk to anyone or make eye contact, and should go crawl in a hole.
6. Upward Turn: Two down is not that bad.
7. Acceptance and Hope: It's just one game and there is always next week, next game, and next tournament.

So yes goalie moms do go through the seven stages of grief. Now it's time for me to set up a goalie mom grief counseling group. Going to need some wine!

## Goalies, So Misunderstood

"To be great is to be misunderstood," or so said Ralph Waldo Emerson in his seminal work, *Self Reliance.* In it, he referenced everyone from Socrates to Galileo and Isaac Newton as individuals once thought as "too out there" for the mainstream.

In hockey, when it comes to "out there," we all immediately think of goalies. You have to be just a little bit "off" to sign up for a position like that. So how do you handle it when your little Brodeur wants to suit up between the pipes?

"Challenges came early," says hockey dad Bill Thieben, whose daughter is a keeper for the Syracuse Nationals.

"The goalie position requires a kid to be a hockey player first—skills, understanding the game, etc. Before that all started to come together, it was brutal. Bad goals were torture."

Thieben recalls his daughter enduring a hailstorm of seventy to eighty shots in a game before. "We always tried to be supportive and made sure that she understood that no matter how bad it got, it was not the end of the world."

Early on, the Thiebens would stand at their daughter's end of the ice for her occasional "look over," as her way of making sure parents were there. Much like teaching your kid to ride a bike, you hang on and hold them up, but then the moment comes when they ride away on their own.

Their teen daughter is now soaring, and does all the analysis for them. "When a bad one gets in, she knows it," says Bill.

"Sometimes a tear is shed, or the stick hits the ice a little harder. But the emotional meltdowns don't occur. She, and conversely we, let it go."

You won't find Sharon Enck in the shadows of an ice rink, though. The Arizona goalie mom blogger sits at center ice with other team parents.

"You can't preach, 'It's a team sport,' when you are huddled in a corner muttering to yourself. Plus, by doing that, you are feeding in to the whole 'goalies and goalie parents are crazy' thing—which we kind of are, but still . . ."

While it may seem goalie parents are teetering on the edge of madness, the complexity of the position can cause disconnects on a team. It's natural for parents to take pity on the goalie parent. Yes, it's expensive. There's stress and tension. But there's also a ton of pride.

"That glow she gets when she's played her hardest and knows she did well. Knowing that she plays the toughest position on the team, has survived several losing seasons, and still comes back for more because she loves it and won't give up," says Enck.

While it's easy for pride to become bruised, goalies also have a certain amount of pride from the bruises earned between the pipes. Enck says she and her daughter name them after whoever gave it to her!

Enck and Thieben have also discovered that their kids learn to deal with life's mental challenges.

"It sounds corny," says Thieben, "but it has helped to build and shape her character, helping to make her a confident and independent young lady in every part of her life. We are not exactly sure what drives her, but something does."

Self reliance: it doesn't seem "too out there." Guess sometimes we just misunderstand.

## Advice to New Goalie Parents

*By Diane Pelton*

As I sat down to think of what advice to give to goalie parents just starting out, my first though was, "Save up your money!" In all seriousness, start by realizing your son or daughter is taking on one of the most demanding, high-pressure positions in all of sports. When a goalie makes a mistake, it ends up on the scoreboard for all to see. They make split-second decisions that immediately affect the outcome of the game. I have learned many things watching my eldest boy, Jacob, grow both as a young man and goaltender.

## Be Seen and Not Heard

One of Jacob's favorite goalie coaches (Mitch Korn) always starts his camps by talking to parents and telling them to be "seen and not heard." I have witnessed many goalie parents walking from end to end, standing behind their goalie, watching every move, or shouting from the stands. Can you imagine going about your day with someone watching over your shoulder? So why would you want to do it to your child? Sit in the stands and resist the temptation to yell out, "watch out," or "pay attention," or, "you should have had that one!" If your goalie is looking at you, they are not focused on the play in front of them.

Realize right from the start that a shutout is hard to come by, and it's not all about the goalie. Good defense has a lot to do with how "good" your goalie looks. At first, when he was young, my son thought he should stop every puck and would get upset when he didn't. Over the years he has learned that his goal is to keep his team in the game as long as possible, giving them a chance to win, by not giving up any "soft goal."

Goals will happen, and when they do, help your goalie to develop mental strategies to put it behind them and focus on the next shot. Once the puck is in the net, getting upset and losing focus isn't going to change anything. Changes are good, the game is not over, and the best goalies are the one that can keep their focus.

## *The Three Things Rule*

One way parents can help their goalie is by keeping track of what type of goal was scored on them. If they are struggling with a particular skill or type of shot, a pattern will emerge and your goalie will know what to work on during practice. As they get older, they can do this for themselves, but they might need help talking through "how could I have played that differently?" Encourage post game analysis, but don't turn it into a lecture in the van on the way home. Be honest. Tell them when they play great, but also tell them when they could have played better. When Jacob was young, his dad and I had the "three things rule." After a game, we would tell Jacob two things we saw that we thought he could have done better and one thing he did well. Eventually, this changed into asking him the three things he thought about the game. Don't let your goalie play the blame game! They are the last line of defense, regardless of mistakes the team has made. Once the puck gets to them, it is their job to try to keep the puck out of the net. Another part of the blame game is learning to ignore comments from other parents. It's tough to watch a game when your child is having an off day in the net, let alone listen to others comment on how your kid looks like Swiss cheese today. Remember, every player has a bad day now and then. Keep it in perspective and the next game will be better. Yes, sometimes it's hard to watch. We want to protect them. But chances are, if your child has chosen to become a goalie, they are much stronger than you may realize. Sit back, relax, and enjoy the game . . . for what it's worth!

## Ways to Be a Saner Goalie Parent

*By Sharon Enck*

"You don't have to be crazy to play goal, but it helps." —Bernie Parent

No truer sentiment has been uttered in the world of hockey and it applies to goalie parents too. What other position on the team carries that kind of pressure, and visibility? Crazy doesn't have to be part of the job description though.

How can you achieve a more Zen state of mind with all that nuttiness floating around the net? Here are few suggestions from a veteran:

### Don't, under Any Circumstances, Stand behind Your Goalie's Net

I've been there, I've done it. It is a never a good idea unless you want more gray hair, a nervous tick, and nausea. Trust me, they don't want you behind the net analyzing every move they make either. Go make friends with the other parents at center ice, you will thank me.

### Keep Those Post game Post Mortems to a Maximum of Ten Minutes

It isn't healthy to keep rehashing things that would've, could've, and should've been. It'll make you both nuts. No more than ten minutes . . . set a timer if you must!

### Ignore Your Inner Statistician

I know parents who check their kid's stats after every game. And tournaments? They huddle around the results sheet on the wall like bees around a beehive. Calculating goal differentials, devising strategy on who needs to win or lose what for their team to be in the playoffs or championship game. And then? They tell their goalie about it—talk about pressure! Balancing my bank account after paying hockey fees and paying for equipment is all the math I need to do in a season.

## *Other Parents Are Not Your Enemies*

It's easy to fall into the mindset that all parents are judging your goalie with every bad goal or loss but it just isn't so. Well, at least not all of them. So, like I said earlier, go make some friends! Sit with them at center ice, and root for the whole team. It will take your mind (ever so slightly) off what is happening in the net. The bonus is that once they know you better it will be harder for them to smack talk when things don't go your goalie's way. Hockey parents can be really awesome, let them prove it!

It's not easy to be the parent of the most visible member of the team but it carries a great honor and privilege. And if none of my tips work, you can always just embrace the crazy and start muttering under your breath during every game.

# 20

## KEYS TO KEEPING
## KIDS SAFE ON THE ICE

**S**oon after our son started playing high school hockey, we added two items as household staples: ice and ibuprofen. A bigger, faster, stronger kid meant bigger, faster, stronger falls and hits. Sometimes I could see the hits coming and would watch with my eyes wide shut.

Whether your kid is a dangler or a ham and egger, there's always a risk of injury. But the same can be said for any sport your son or daughter is involved in.

So the real question is, how do we protect them?

Let's start at the top. There's no such thing as a concussion-proof helmet, but a helmet that fits well and meets the certification criteria is definitely a great start.

Dr. Alan Ashare, the head of USA Hockey's Safety and Protective Equipment Committee, says helmets have a six-year life span from the date they are manufactured, not the date they are sold, and must have a current HECC sticker.

"The helmet should not be able to move around on the head," Ashare says.

Sure, we all want to save money, especially at a time when our kids are growing like weeds, but it's important that every piece of equipment is properly fitted.

"Make sure pants are long enough," advises Caryn Hammond, a hockey mom from Vernon Hills, Illinois. "In squirts and peewees, they tend to grow up and not out, so it's easy to realize your kids' pants are way too short, even though they still 'fit,' leaving lots of vulnerable area for pucks and sticks to hit."

Perhaps the biggest thing a parent can do to keep their kids safe is to learn the signs and symptoms of concussions and understand concussion management. Online programs like the Centers for Disease Control website (cdc.gov/concussion/sports) and the National Federation of High Schools website (NFHS .org) are good resources for players, coaches, and parents.

Beyond the equipment, there's something even more basic and so essential to keeping our kids safe. It's called respect. That includes respecting the rules, opponents, referees, and coaches. It also means playing the game under control both physically and emotionally.

"If you respect the game, it will make it more enjoyable and safer to play," says Rochester Institute of Technology Coach Wayne Wilson.

And if you wear the required equipment properly, and you play the game the way it is intended to be played—by the rules that are in place at all levels—the game is very safe and fun to play.

Hockey is fun. It's up to all of us to make sure the game is safe for our kids.

# 21

## CONCUSSION CARE IS CHALLENGING

**T**here was a time when I rarely heard about concussions. But now, rarely a season goes by where I don't witness a significant injury or meet a parent whose child recently suffered one.

Surprisingly, even the most well-protected players are not exempt from harm, as West Springfield, Massachusetts, hockey mom Tiffany Basile found out in the hardest way possible for a parent.

Her daughter Kaylee's talent and passion as a goalie was putting her on the college recruiting radar. And then, during a game, an opposing team stormed her net, delivering an unexpected blow to her head. A concussion put her out for a week, with lingering effects causing depression and anxiety.

A year later, a second hit to the head during a practice only made matters worse.

Kaylee's eyes couldn't follow a pen, her balance was off, and she failed every computer brain test. She suffered a seizure during an

MRI and results confirmed what her mom had feared: the risk of further injury on the ice was too significant to continue playing.

"Breaking the news that she could never play again was horrible and heartbreaking," says Basile.

But for the sake of Kaylee's health, there simply was no other option.

"It was best for her to steer clear of any activities that can risk more harm and injury. Her health and safety are first."

Basile advises parents to educate themselves on the signs and symptoms of concussions and to share this knowledge with their athletes.

"I'm thankful to have my daughter with me after all she has been through."

Hockey dad Greg Jewett, a physical education teacher at the Christian Brothers Academy in Syracuse, raises concerns about protocol for players returning to the ice after a concussion. Last season's peewee coach was very supportive when his son, Alec, missed practices after suffering from a mild concussion. But do all coaches feel that way?

Youth hockey programs are not monitored by schools, and the policies within these programs regarding concussions and testing vary. This lack of consistency may lead to avoidable harm.

"I think that youth hockey organizations should adopt the impact testing that high schools use as a way to measure brain activity and if and when a player is ready to return," Jewett says. "But with no trainers on site and no testing in place, this is a problem for youth hockey going forward."

He raises a valid point. When there is no organizational protocol in place, players may find themselves prematurely pressured to return to the ice by teammates, parents, and coaches.

Concussion care is challenging. Even the highest levels of professional sports are re-examining the way they treat head trauma.

Thankfully, USA Hockey provides online resources to help parents and players. Take the time to educate yourself, and share your knowledge with others. Work with your teams to develop safety protocols that don't rush kids back to the ice too quickly. And always remember to seek timely medical treatment.

So while we can't wrap our kids in that bubble wrap, we can continue to wrap our minds around safety procedures and prevention.

No room for bullies in hockey. *Credit:* Darren Gygi

# 22

## DON'T LET BULLYING TAKE THE FUN OUT OF THE GAME

---

**O**ne of the great lessons gained by participating in sports is learning how to overcome adversity. But sometimes the greatest adversity doesn't come on the ice from the opposing team, but instead from teammates in the locker room.

A bully can make life miserable for any player who is scapegoated, teased, or ridiculed. A team's rituals can also cross the line into hazing. These acts call for vigilance on the part of parents, and, as always, begins with a coach who's tuned into his team.

"No drama." That has always been the number one locker room rule for Skaneateles (New York) High School Athletic Director Mike Major, who counts on his team captains to help reinforce the strict no bullying stance on and off the ice.

While captains serve an important mentoring role, it's the coach who needs to monitor the pulse of the team. They should keep an ear to the ground on the bench and in the locker room to create an atmosphere of trust and respect.

"A coach needs to set up consequences for bullying and enforce them—even if it means benching or terminating the best player on his team," says Dan Saferstein, team psychologist for USA Hockey's National Team Development Program. "Bullying doesn't just hurt the victims of bullying. It weakens the entire team and creates a culture of fear and cowardice."

Stacey Wierl, a Westchester County youth hockey coach, believes coaches, players, and sometimes parents have a hard time differentiating between a prank, a joke, and an act of bullying.

Wierl recalls a bullying incident involving a peewee skater, who was a small and somewhat reserved easy target. His teammates threw his sneakers in the toilet after one practice. Swift action followed, with the coaches suspending the players who were part of the prank. Once the suspensions were over, the coach hosted team dinners and fun off-ice sessions to create a strong team bond, which prevented any additional situations.

Social media should also be a huge concern when preventing bullying, as it can often take bullying to another level.

"If bullying is happening in the locker room, you can almost guarantee it is happening via text, Twitter, Instagram, or Facebook," Wierl says. "Coaches must acknowledge this possibility and encourage parents to check phones and be aware of these dangers."

In my personal experience, on my daughter's team, we assign a parent to collect all the phones before players go into the locker room before every practice or game, in an effort cut down on the chances of a theft and inappropriate snapchats.

Bullying in athletics is real and cuts across all levels. When not addressed, it can quickly cause its victims to loathe not just the harassment, but the sport itself.

## DON'T LET BULLYING TAKE THE FUN OUT OF THE GAME

"The scars of bullying can run deep," says Saferstein, who encourages parents to be vigilant to the signs and symptoms that their child is being subjected to bullying.

"I would do whatever it takes to empower your child and not let a bully poison his or her love for hockey."

Resist the temptation to coddle your kid. *Credit:* Darren Gygi

# 23

## HOCKEY PARENTS WALK A FINE LINE BETWEEN CODDLING AND CARING

**W**e sign our kids up to play sports because we want them to learn and grow, to know what it's like to be a part of team, to work hard to achieve a goal, and to learn how to deal with adversity.

But sometimes it's difficult for a parent to stand back and watch the learning process unfold. It's part of our parental DNA to feel that we should do whatever we can to help them. But there is a fine line between coddling and caring.

Take the skate-lacing dilemma, for instance. There's going to come a time when you're no longer allowed in the locker room, and your child is going to have to tighten those laces on their own.

The same goes for carrying your child's hockey bag. This was a huge pet peeve of my son's former coach, who wasn't shy to take a parent to task for slinging their kid's bag on their shoulders.

Hockey mom Linda Aitcheson has a rule for her nine-year-old goalie: if you wear it, you wheel it.

"As a parent and coach, having children tie their own skates and carry their own bags [when they are old enough to do so] is not tough love at all," says Matt Sweeney, a Baldwinsville, New York, coach. "It is teaching them to be responsible and independent—two important life skills."

Sweeney has a point: by doing everything for your child, especially when they are perfectly capable of doing it themselves, you teach your son or daughter to rely on others for everything. Eventually, they'll lose confidence in themselves and you'll end up with a child who may not be capable of standing on his or her own two feet.

As Mary Gaspirini, a veteran Syracuse, New York, hockey mom, sagely says, "We are parents first, and one of the primary goals of being a parent is to teach our children how to take care of themselves."

For example, when it comes to your child learning how to lace up his or her own skates, Gaspirini suggests trying a few open skates first. It's a great environment for trying to learn this skill and is stress-free as opposed to right before a game or practice.

Sometimes it's best to just sit back and let the game itself reveal something about your little one, say, when you see your child struggling with others on the team.

By letting them figure things out for themselves, you're helping your young hockey player develop into a confident, capable kid that you'll be proud of.

"Again, this is a great opportunity to teach life skills such as how to be assertive and how to properly resolve conflict," Sweeney says.

So remember, the next time you're about to hoist your kid's bag on your own shoulder, ask yourself if you're really lightening their load further on down the line.

# 24

## AVOIDING THE CRACKS IN THE ICE: A FORTE OF SEASONED HOCKEY MOMS

**L**ong before I understood the breadth of my super powers as a hockey mom, I was foiled by that malodorous miscreant also known as the hockey bag.

Able to fell foes with a single whiff, my newfound nemesis would eventually be defeated thanks to a strict ritual of cleaning and airing of all gear after each game and practice.

If only I had known hockey bags and foul odors don't have to skate together, I might have spared my singed nostrils a lot of pain.

Sometimes it takes time to learn these hard lessons, as most hockey moms can attest.

Grizzled veterans can always spot a newbie as she enters the rink for the first time with that deer-in-the-headlights look on her face and think, *Oh, if she only knew . . .*

It's a learning process that doesn't happen overnight, and sometimes it doesn't come cheap.

"It requires using vacation days from work, missing birthday parties, and paying extra costs besides fees and equipment," says Syracuse Nationals hockey mom Lauren Kochian.

Eventually she ditched the guilt and realized that it takes a village to survive the season.

"A hockey team is truly a family and you shouldn't feel like you have to be at every practice and game," she says. "Let others pitch in and reciprocate. It's a good way for kids to see that teamwork off the ice."

There are a lot of sacrifices that come with being a hockey mom, but it can be well worth it. Just ask University of Pittsburgh hockey mom Karen Palonis, who found out last year that the rewards are well worth it, especially when it comes in the form of a national championship.

"That was an amazing feeling and great to share that joy with my son," Palonis says.

It's also great to share that feeling with others, as my sister, Teresa Marzec, a hockey coach from Saugerties, New York, can attest. "Getting involved made me appreciate the game so much more," Teresa says. "There's great satisfaction in knowing you've helped make the season more memorable for the kids and parents."

And that's what it's all about.

Do we make mistakes? Sure. Do we look back on those *Duh!* moments and wonder, *What was I thinking?* Absolutely.

But just like our kids on the ice, we figure it out. And as my sister says, the rewards far outweigh the trials and tribulations.

"Would you have traded a second of it?" she asks.

Nope. Not one second.  Amen sister.

Q: What advice would you give to new hockey parents?

A: Be patient, be positive, and make sure your child is having fun. You want them to learn to love the game, embrace the camaraderie, and create memories that will last a lifetime. Also, volunteer with your child's team and/or the hockey association. This will ensure you are more involved and understand that it is more than just hockey—it's about life lessons that are instilled in our youth each and every day. Trust your coach, listen to your child, and encourage team. —*Debbie Barnes, Syracuse Nationals mom, LaFargeville, New York*

A: Hockey will become your life. But, your family will grow immensely and you will have the best support system for all aspects of life. You will have a better relationship with your children than you ever thought possible. —*Mike Strykowski, Syracuse Nationals dad, Pine City, New York*

# 25

# WATER MOM AND OTHER ROOKIE MISTAKES

## By Sharon Enck

**I was never** a sports person. In high school I played one season of softball and after a barrage of bruises on my shins as a second basewoman and one lucky home run, I decided to retire. So, when my daughter begged me for a year to learn how to play hockey, I was pretty hesitant even though we had started being big fans. As I told her back then, "I like your teeth in your head."

Persistence does pay off and eventually I gave in. I found out about the Kids First program (now the Little Howlers*), which allows kids from ages four to eight to try hockey for free. It consists of one session per week for four weeks, borrowed equipment included.

*Why not?,* I thought. Little did I know that I would be entering a whole new world.

I can tell you from experience that players on the ice aren't the only ones making the mistakes. As a new sports mom, I was ignorant to the delicate balance of cool hockey mom and annoyingly overprotective. Case in point, the very first day of my daughter's hockey clinic, I hovered by the glass like a puppy. I felt this was somewhat forgivable with it being her first time and all. Lots of other parents were doing the same.

Unfortunately I didn't stop there. Feeling that my daughter, after being out on the ice for approximately ten minutes, was dehydrated to the point of a slow death, I waved her over, water bottle in hand. It took only twice for the coach to pick up on this and he discreetly screamed cross ice, "Hey Water Mom, she's fine!" Let the embarrassment begin. This became, for the rest of the clinic and her private lessons, my inescapable nickname, much to my daughter's amusement.

It wasn't my first mistake, nor was it my last.

Learning to have to put goalie pads on a six-year-old was probably more frustrating than the labor it took to bring her into the world. Cussing and sweating, it took me nearly thirty minutes just to figure it all out. I strapped her in nice and tight and sent her out.

She dropped to her knees and couldn't get back up. She lay there on the ice flailing like a fish out of water and I had no idea why. Her coach skates by, grabs her by the back of the breezers, and sets her on her skates.

"Hey Water Mom, her pads are too tight!"

Basically I had strapped what probably felt like wooden boards to her legs, making it nearly impossible for her to bend and get up. Once I looked at the back of more experienced goalies, I realized just how loose those straps had to be behind the legs.

Oops.

More tips: you never call them cute, take pictures of them in the locker room, or fuss over their war wounds. You need to make "suck it up" part of your vocabulary.

Even rooting for your team has its own set of rules. Cheering is acceptable until your team is annihilating the other. Then you do a quiet golf clap or nothing at all. Having been on the receiving end of many a beating, it just stings to hear the other team's parent go berserk when they score that tenth goal in your team's scoreless game. Especially when it is your goalie giving them up!

The experienced parent mumbles under their breath and says things like "set it up," "get to the net," or "watch that back door," while the inexperienced parent is hooting, hollering, and yelling things like "skate!" and "get it out." The ones who also wave to their kid on the ice, oh yeah I have done it.

While these weren't my last mistakes, we've made it to our ninth season (and yes, all goalie years) and that's not too bad for a non-sports person.

For more information about the Little Howlers, please visit: http://azice.com/gilbert/hockey/little-howlers-free-hockey/

Hockey parents can get in on the game too. *Credit:* Darren Gygi

# 26

## HOCKEY MOMS WON'T LET KIDS HAVE ALL THE FUN

**Any hockey fan** knows the Great One's most famous words: "You miss 100 percent of the shots you don't take."

It's a nice sentiment, but for those of us who live in reality, sometimes we're just too old to start putting the proverbial puck on net.

Enter the Nightmares, true dream chasers, who believe it is never too late to try something new.

This mom squad is from Saugerties, New York, and includes my sister, Teresa Marzec. She helps lead the pack. With assists from the Saugerties youth hockey club and Kiwanis Ice Arena director Robbie Kleemann, the moms were able to get a low-cost adult program going, with a weekly practice and six games.

"I love, love, love hockey," says Donna Cohn Viertel, the team's goalie. "Playing it and watching it."

While her team thinks of her as a standout keeper, she is a self-proclaimed "stand-up" goalie, which she blames on bad knees and advanced age. Emotions also get the best of her.

"I cry when I play badly," she admits.

No longer content to watch from the bleachers, these moms have also gained a new perspective for the game. Sitting in the stands, yelling at our kids, shaking our heads when they miss a pass, that all stops.

"I think I've always appreciated the complexity of the game," says Kat Marrinan. "However, stepping on the ice myself certainly opened my eyes to the extreme discipline involved in simultaneously skating and puck-handling, while dodging opposing players."

Many have also discovered that hockey provides a better full-body workout than their local spinning or Pilates classes, and is a whole lot more fun.

"Many of the women that play in my clinics and leagues have dropped their health club memberships," says Mike Curti, who has been running clinics for women players in the Twin Cities for the past twelve years.

"For many, this is the first team sport they have participated in. It has been a joy for me to watch friendships form from the many women that have come together for my clinics.

Many of these women have moved on from the clinics to form teams that play in area leagues.

Marrinan encourages all women—not just hockey moms—to lace up skates, borrow some equipment, and pick up a stick.

"It's not for everyone, but if you don't take the chance, you never know," she says. "You might be turning your back on the greatest adventure, and love, of your life."

In other words, just as any hockey coach will tell you, good things happen when you put the puck on net.

# 27

## HOW TO SHOOT AND SCORE GOOD GAME PHOTOS

---

**We know how** challenging it is for our kids to handle a stick and puck while maneuvering around the ice to score a goal. It can be challenging for those of us in the stands with a camera, eager to catch all the great action and reaction. Ice arenas are far from ideal settings to capture those magical moments, but with a few tricks of the trade, you may be able to snap some keepsake shots.

### Ask the Photographers

Photojournalist Mark Folsom has kindly agreed to assist those of us in the amateur photography league with tips on how to shoot like a pro.

Q: What advice do you have to help us capture the action of this fast-moving sport?

A: Find a good place to set yourself up to capture the action. Be as close to the ice as you can. It's great for getting the close-ups of action shots of your favorite player, or go to the middle of the stands to cover as much ice as possible. Also position yourself for viewing both goals they should be equal distance from your lens. Using a lens with a 135 to 400 mm focal length with a lens opening of 2.8 should be sufficient. Try using a higher ISO setting for the camera; 800 to 3200 modern cameras are pretty good at that level. ISO is the sensitivity to the light. Anticipate the action and focus on the eyes and get ready to press the shutter release at the peak of action.

Q: Light in a hockey rink is awful. Should we use a flash?

A: Yes! A powerful flash is a good idea, but not a necessity. The light reflecting from the ice is a problem, because it tricks your camera into thinking it is brighter than it actually is; you need to compensate for that by telling the camera to open up the amount of light it lets in by a full stop or two. You could use the flash if you have a powerful external flash unit because the distance the light has to travel to get to your subject is greater.

Birmingham, Michigan, hockey mom/photographer Liz Weidner also recommends that you ask the rink manager what type of lights are used in the arena, whether they are incandescent or fluorescent, to help you obtain the proper settings for your camera.

Q: How do we get our pictures to be bright and crisp, instead of blurry and grainy?

A: Use a fast lens to get the most amount of light into the camera and a high shutter speed to freeze the action as much as possible. A shutter speed of 1/250th a second or greater should be enough. The higher speed helps to freeze the action. Fast ISO also helps, but try and stay under 3200 ISO. Only the more advanced and expensive cameras are good above this sensitivity level.

Q: Where are the best spots in a rink to get good shots?

A: I would try down by the glass boards (if it's clean). That way you can be close to the action. Try the corners, or behind the goal is another good place to position yourself and let the action come to you. Even though you don't have the big lens, there is plenty you can do to take some really good sports photos. Afterwards, in post editing processing of your images, use a good photo editing program to crop and zoom in to the best composition. If you don't have a tripod, make yourself into one; lock your elbows in and lean up against something.

## *Here's Your Photography Game Plan*

- Get in position
- Work out in advance where you should be
- Anticipate the action
- Try to predict what's going to happen so you're ready at the crucial moment
- Use your zoom telephoto for shots that put you at the thick of the action
- Use fast shutter speeds
- Increase your ISO if you can
- Keeping shooting—set your camera to shoot a continuous series of pictures in a single purse
- Zoom in as far as you can; be beware of using digital zoom because it may not give you the image quality you'll need if you are going to crop
- Use a good photo editing program

Liz Weidner also recommends that you not delete any photos until you have zoomed and cropped the final image. "With huge files sizes, sometimes the smallest thing can become the best picture," says Weidner.

Not all good sports photos have to be of the action of the game itself. You might get some surprisingly great pictures if you turn your back on the main event and capture the reactions of the crowd. It really works if you're able to catch the expression of parents and fans at a key moment. Or, look for those candid shots of your kids tense with concentration, exhausted at the end of the game, or enjoying the moment and the sheer joy of just being on the ice.

Hotels don't always roll out the welcome mat for hockey families. "Hotel Horror Stories." *Credit:* Darren Gygi

# 28

## HOW TO TURN THE PAGE ON HOTEL HOCKEY HORROR STORIES

---

**O**ver the years, my family has had some fun times on the road. We've also had our fair share of hotel horror stories. Like the time our team of twelve-year-old boys got the bright idea to see how many hockey players it would take to lift a heavy glass table in the lobby. Let's just say that eight wasn't enough.

The first time checking into a hotel as newbie hockey parents took my husband and me by surprise. Signing waivers, reading a lengthy list of rules, and being given a lecture all clued me in to the contentious relationship between hockey families and hotels. While some hotels are more hockey family–friendly than others, there are certain rules that need to be followed to keep the welcome mat from being pulled out from under your team.

Before checking in, check out advice from families who've been there, done that.

- Make sure the hotel has a common area or a conference room you can use for kids and parents. It is a win-win for families and the hotel. —*Mike Carni, Lysander, New York*
- Spend time researching family-friendly restaurants and places to visit away from the rink. Be sure to ask about popular local fare. —*Mike Marsallo, Lysander, New York*
- Depending on the players' level, no swimming before games. Potluck dinners are cost effective and a great bonding experiece. The movie *Miracle* is a must. Hold a talent contest with players and coaches and give everyone five minutes each to sing, tell jokes, magic tricks, etc. It was the highlight of our season. —*Jeffrey Slattery, Osseo, Minnesota*
- Secure a conference-style room where kids can play until curfew without disturbing hotel guests, and parents can mingle and share food. An end-of-the-season slide show with pictures and video clips will trigger laughter and good memories. —*Stephanie Secreto, New Windsor, New York*
- It's always good to find a hotel with a bar/restaurant. Free breakfast is a bonus. —*Caryn Hammond, Lake Zurich, Illinois*
- No swimming in between games. No mini sticks in hallways when on a floor with non-hockey families, who may not want to step out of their rooms and into the middle of a game. —*Alyssa Proud, Oswego, New York*
- Remind your players, and parents, that you're not just representing yourself when you travel to tournaments; you're representing your entire association. Acting up in a hotel could impact other teams in your association down the road. —*Gene Firefly, Sheboygan, Wisconsin*

## HOW TO TURN THE PAGE ON HOTEL HOCKEY HORROR STORIES

My son, in college as of this writing, doesn't remember as much about the wins and losses of road games as he does the knee-hockey contests, pool challenges, and pizza parties. And of course he remembers the sound that a glass table makes when it hits the lobby floor. It's definitely one memory I wish that I could erase.

Holidays are often spent on the road. *Credit:* Darren Gygi

# 29

# HOCKEY FOR THE HOLIDAYS: A SPECIAL TIME FOR FAMILIES

**The smell was** the first thing that got me—an odd mixture of Crock-Pot ham, scalloped potatoes, and hotel cleaning supplies.

Hours earlier, I had spent the evening attempting to convince my daughter, Sophia—eight years old at the time—that yes, the Easter bunny would find us, even in Canada.

That was the year Mr. Cottontail climbed up the ranks of holiday favorites, as he somehow managed to sneak into a strange hotel room, deliver a big basket of chocolate goodies, and hide dozens of colored eggs in the hallways for egg hunts.

When you're a hockey family, you learn to create holiday traditions on the fly.

We found a local church for services and then enjoyed that unconventional Easter buffet with the other families on our team. We didn't allow hockey to usurp our time with family, friends, or faith.

Hockey families are always on the go during the season, especially in November. The four-day holiday is typically a time when many families forgo the traditional turkey dinners for Thanksgiving tournaments.

While Oswego, New York, hockey mom Jackie Reilly has spent nearly every Thanksgiving in recent memory at tournaments, they are still treasured times for her family.

"We have dinner Thursday and then off we go," Reilly says. "Not one of us feels bad about it. Is that wrong? We are a hockey family through and through and our family and friends all know and respect that. I truly believe hockey has helped us to be more of a family."

Syracuse Nationals dad John Manzi agrees. His two boys have never complained about leaving on any holiday.

"They absolutely love packing the car and taking those long journeys either to Boston or Canada," he says. "The bond that takes place between any hockey parent and child starts with those trips."

Hilary Gorlin will always remember the high school tournament that fell during Hanukkah when she brought a Menorah to the hotel.

"To this day, it is a really special memory for me, bringing my team together to celebrate something that many of them didn't know a lot about," says the coach with the Rose City Hockey Club of Portland, Oregon.

Sharing a holiday on the road requires some planning. You may want to consider booking hotel rooms with kitchenettes to allow you to prepare even a modest feast. Manzi suggests organizing a team dinner, rather than making separate reservations at restaurants. With a little planning, he says, you can make it feel somewhat like a holiday that is celebrated at home.

"After all, hockey players and their parents are always one big family through the season," Manzi says.

And as long as you're surrounded by family, there's no road holiday that can't be enjoyed.

# 30

## PROPER PLANNING MAY BE THE BIGGEST PRESENT YOU CAN GIVE YOURSELF

**W**hat **words come** to mind when you think of the holidays? Peace, love, and joy? Or travel, tournaments, and stress?

Hockey families execute a delicate act of balancing school events, holiday parties, family gatherings, practices, games, and tournaments. It's as stressful as guarding a one-goal lead in a playoff game.

The holidays are a lot like hockey in another way: winning efforts come to those who plan.

So here are a few tips from my life and the lives of my hockey friends:

- Having a visual game plan can be one of the best ways to keep the family a little more sane and organized during crazy holidays. I use a dry-erase calendar to keep my home team in line. Place it in a high-traffic area such as the kitchen or family room. That way your family can see what's coming up, when to say no and work together to tackle the many tasks of the season. Mark down work, school, games, family commitments, schedule holiday shopping, baking, and even gift wrapping.

- You can count on conflicts in the schedule so setting up a car pool might be the next best thing to Santa's sleigh. Parents are always willing to pitch in and help shuttle the kids to their destinations. Make sure you return the favor.

- Make your list, check it twice, and, as hockey friend Caroline Stanistreet suggests, do the mom and dad timeshare. One parent goes to the games and the other stays home to clean or cook. As long as you are both there for the championship game, your kids will understand.

- I admire Skaneateles, New York, hockey mom Shannon Proud, too, for always finding unique gifts at shops near the rinks. Her kids get their practice, and she painlessly whittles down holiday wish lists. Online shopping on the smartphone or iPad during intermissions can give you that home team advantage, too.

- Lose the guilt and cheat. Go ahead and cut corners during this crazy season. If the holiday tournament calls for parents to supply food, pick up a couple of pizzas or buy one of those family-sized frozen macaroni-and-cheese dinners. Doctor it up with a little seasoning and toss it in a Crock-Pot. You'll satisfy a hungry crowd, save time, and make money for the team.

A lot of planning and a little compromising can go a long way and help you keep the "ho ho ho" in the holiday.

# 31

## AVOIDING TOURNAMENT TURMOIL

---

**The to-do list** is usually a long one right before a tournament.

Confirm hotel reservations? Check. Get directions to the rinks? Check. Find the bathing suits, knee hockey sticks, cooler, and *Miracle* DVD? Check.

When the day comes to pack up the car and begin the journey, don't you wish you could leave that bag of anxiety behind?

As Rink Rat Tournament Chair Bill Andrews points out, there are plenty of ways for parents and coaches to cut down on tournament turmoil. The biggest thing is to remember that the focus should be on making it a fun and positive experience.

Finding a tournament that offers a balance of fair competition and fun should be first priority. Hockey family–friendly hotels and entertainment during down times are also a huge plus.

Andrews is a fan of tournaments that offer some type of skills competitions or other fun on-ice activities to help take the focus off of the scoreboard.

"It challenges the kids, keeps them together, and lets them earn more participation-type trophies," he says.

There are other ways to keep costs down and kids entertained, too.

"Bring a Nerf football or tennis ball for the pool, and keep the knee hockey and Crock-Pot rooms going," he says. "That will keep the kids still, instead of running the hallways where things can get loud and accidentally broken."

The same discipline required on the ice is required away from the rink, too.

"That's important because the kids will exhaust themselves on adrenaline if they don't get a mental rest," says Andrews.

Coaches will need help from parents to keep the curfew on pool times and making sure no one is left out or left behind.

While it's natural for nasty nerves to strike when taking on new teams in a new town, they don't have to take over. Cue the *Rocky* music. Don't discount the power of a good movie.

"Watching movies like *Rudy* or *Miracle* can help kids gain perspective," Andrews says.

Of course good coaching comes into play too.

"Do what works for you all season long," he says. "Being upbeat and excited to play the competition takes away from the fear of being David against Goliath."

So what if the kids are getting clobbered?

"Just have fun and try to win the little battles. Win the faceoff, have a shift where you get it into their zone, get two shots off in a shift. Make it a manageable task, not a mountain," Andrews says.

So, if during the next tournament, your kids are up against intense competitive pressure, do remember to sweat the small stuff.

# 32

## SO YOU WANT TO HOST A
## HOCKEY TOURNAMENT

**S**hould your organization run a tournament? The most important question to ask is, can you run a good one? Bad ones can hurt your reputation, leave you exhausted, and possibly in debt. They're a lot of work, but with the right guidance, motives, and preparation, hosting a weekend extravaganza could end up feeling as rewarding as a tournament hat trick.

The team behind the successful Troy Albany Hockey Association's Rink Rat Tournament says your motives need to be genuine. The goal should never be "doing it because we always do it" or "do it to make money."

"If you do it for the right reasons, giving your own kids a home tourney and your guests a good experience when they are in town, the profits and all the rest will take care of themselves," says Rink Rat Tournament Director Bill Andrews.

### Decisions, Decisions

Andrews always asks himself what teams look for when they are picking a tournament to attend. There are different types.

"When I host one for a highly competitive AAA level—those teams are looking for a different experience than a House or recreational level team. The idea is to be cognizant of the focus and interest of the target group and to provide them with an experience as close to what they are looking for," advises Andrews.

Andrews also points to the importance of knowing your audience. "Some want scouting opportunities—so competitive teams and reaching out to schools is a must. Some want hockey bling. If that's the case, offer hats, bracelets, sweatshirts, apparel as much as possible. Some want pool time and knee hockey. Some are all about playing teams from as far away as possible; some want only the standard one game Friday, two on Saturday, one on Sunday, and crossovers. If you think about the population you are trying to serve and work to serve that group as best you can; then, you end up with a good tourney."

Andrews has learned hockey teams are willing to pay more for quality. "People don't like being shaken down or hit up at every corner. Everyone remembers the great games, the best experiences, and the most horrific events. Everything else is a blur and fading memory over the marathon that is the youth hockey experience. A tourney that strives to create a positive, memorable experience will undoubtedly do that—when there is a conscious aim and objective to achieve that result. The hockey community is small. Coaches in regions all know each other. Coaches that coach certain levels—like the girls programs—are mainstays. And they talk to each other. Give a memorable experience and word spreads."

## Little Things Can Make You Big

Andrews credits much of the success of the annual Rink Rat Tournament to paying attention to details, "There are certain things I do for every tournament that are targeted to connect with the expectations of the incoming teams. All in all, those things are simply paying attention to little details that are simply designed to give your guests the best experience possible."

According to Andrews, some of those things could include having honor guards or bagpipers at the championship rounds and having singers to sing both Canadian and American national anthems. "Some tourneys it's skills sessions, always it's a great raffle, no gate fee, giveaways, good competition (with a concerted effort toward having parity in divisions), good apparel, and extras like discount tickets to nearby D1 games, bonfires, and fireworks," says Andrews.

## Family Focus

Vice President of Operations for the Troy Albany Hockey Association Keith Zimmerman agrees with Bill about the need to focus on the tournament being family friendly throughout, from the rink to the hotels. "We have all been to tourneys where you get your games and leave. It is the extras that make it a memorable experience."

Zimmerman says they've also discovered something pretty big in the Albany area with the smallest and the youngest sets with mite jamborees. "A few years ago with the adoption of cross ice for all of the U8 programs the question arose: 'How do we get these kids out to play other teams?' Yes, there are mite tournaments out there but that is old school when there was full-ice mite A and B teams. It really comes down to coaching ideals and program structure. If you follow USA Hockey, the mites should be all about fun and skill development. No scores should be kept in the games," says Zimmerman. Mite jamborees already have a proven track record with their organization.

Tournaments can be emotional powder kegs, but with the right focus, they can create some dynamite memories that will last your kids a lifetime.

# 33

## TURN A PROFIT AT YOUR TOURNAMENT TABLE

**W**e don't always score the hardware when we host tournaments, but we usually net a nice profit at the parent-manned tables, where we raffle off baskets and offer homemade treats to feed fan appetites. Pulled Pork, walking tacos (no plate needed and all ingredients go right into the chip bags), pork sliders, and every kid's favorite, macaroni and cheese, are always big sellers.

To display the menu, consider using a dry-erase board. Or, raid your kids' room for big art boards to post choices and prices. Crock-Pot dishes are a great way to keep foods hot and fresh, but don't forget that power chord to plug them all in!

An easy way to sweeten the fundraising pot is with lots of sweet treats. Puck-shaped cookies usually sell like hot cakes! Make it a team effort by getting your kids to help you assemble caramel apples, bagged popcorn, or brownies. If you are assigned to cover the morning shifts, your favorite donut shop treats, along with freshly made breakfast pizza, will satisfy stomachs and fill that cash register. Cleverly wrapped fruits and nuts will get gobbled up too. During one of my first tournament experiences, I was surprised to learn just how generous local merchants can be by asking for small donations like a box of donuts, paper products, and pizza in exchange for a little signage or program recognition.

Get creative with your raffle baskets. With a little bit of luck, you just might strike it rich with a lottery basket and really clean up with a bucket of car cleaning suds.

For drinks, buy water in bulk and consider selling cups or small cartons of chocolate milk, plugging in what research says about it being a great snack for athletes after activity.

Struggling for a fresh idea for a raffle basket? I bought more than an arm's length of tickets trying to win the "Hockey Survival Basket" that included:

- Coffee shop gift card
- Fleece blanket
- Coffee
- Coffee thermos
- *Miracle* DVD
- Foot warmers
- Hand warmers
- First aid kit
- Ibuprofen
- Aspirin
- Hand wipes
- Ice scraper

- Sandwich shop gift card
- Chocolate bar
- Water bottle
- Breath mints

All the above ingredients will help any hockey parent make it through a long, cold season!

# 34

## THE CROCK-POT ARMY WAGES WAR AGAINST FAST FOOD PIT STOPS

**Take two parents** who work full time, add hockey-playing children, a cup of after-school activities, a dose of volunteer work, a pound of housework and what have you got? The recipe for a nightly dinner dilemma!

What's a hockey family to do? The Crock-Pot just may ease your hockey season indigestion. Simply dump everything into the slow cooker in the morning, and *Voila!*, you just saved yourself time and money, and whipped up a healthful alternative to the fast food pit stop.

It wasn't hard to recruit Baldwinsville, New York, hockey mom Jackie Waldon to the army of Crock-Pot converts. With four boys to feed, she presses the Crock-Pot into service on a near nightly basis, cooking everything from pulled pork to chicken stew and even breakfast.

"I think for working, single mothers like myself, it is one of the best tools to have for a hot-cooked meal," Jackie says. "When

I work nights, I'll put oatmeal, sliced apples, cinnamon, and sugar and water in the Crock-Pot and breakfast is ready for them in the morning."

Crock-Pot meals can also turn a profit at your tournament table with delightful dishes like pulled pork and macaroni and cheese that provide a better alternative to snack bar chili dogs and nachos.

Syracuse Nationals hockey mom Kim Tretowicz uses her Crock-Pot for team dinners. Her chicken wing dip scores big.

"Although not the healthiest choice, the boys love it," Kim says. "It's a quick and easy appetizer. We had a team dinner in between two games in Rochester. I put it together in the morning and it was steaming ready after our first game with chili, a big tossed salad, and pizza. The kids were able to rest, eat, and then head back to the rink for the second game."

Lysander, New York, hockey mom Jennifer Grinnals turns to the Crock-Pot to save money during tournaments as well.

"Rather than eating out all weekend, we make meals with the Crock-Pot," she says. "Most times the kids would rather spend time in the hotel than be in a restaurant, so it's a win-win for everyone."

Jennifer's tip when cooking ground beef? Brown up a few pounds when time allows, then freeze in one pound packages for quick Crock-Pot meals without the additional prep work.

No question it works for hockey families by adding the key ingredients of comfort and convenience to a long, cold, and sometimes stressful season.

## Big Tip for Eating Out with the Team

Planning is everything when it comes to eating out with the team. It's no fun showing up unannounced at a restaurant with a crowd of parents, siblings, and sixteen sweaty hockey players, especially when you're out of town, between games, and pressed for time.

Our team managers have all been gifted with the knack for knowing how to organize and pick the restaurant that can accommodate a crew of hungry kids and thirsty parents. Calling ahead of time, even a few weeks ahead of time, can spare you headaches and hunger pains.

## Order by Jersey Number

When you're eating out with the team and you don't want to split the bill sixteen ways, ask for separate checks using your player's jersey number. This allows players, parents, and siblings to sit where they want, plus it cuts down on confusion and time of figuring out who owes what. #BestTipEver

# 35

## WHEN HOCKEY HURTS

**I**t was painful to watch when it happened and the recovery was an arduous journey for my peewee hockey boy. His wrist snapped after he flew into the boards, fist first, during a tournament in Niagara Falls. Far from home, we had to take him to an unfamiliar hospital in an unfamiliar city.

It was scary for him and nerve-racking for us, not knowing the doctors, the steps we should be taking, or the road ahead of us. An X-ray confirmed his wrist was broken and his spirit took a hit too. He insisted on staying until the end of the tournament.

His teammates rallied around him and even dedicated their victory to him. That Niagara Falls fracture would be the first in a long line of injuries for our son. Our orthopedic surgeon is now on speed dial, and we learned a lot about injuries, treatment, and prevention.

### Sprains, Strains, and Pain

Treat bruises with RICE: Rest, Ice, Compression, and Elevation. If your child does suffer a sidelining injury, be prepared for a range of emotions which may include anger, sadness, and even depression.

Don't isolate them from teammates and coaches. When injured, my son stayed active with the team, went to the games, and offered defensive strategies from the bench. It wasn't easy and it seemed like the longest season ever, but we stayed positive.

Stress to your kid that they should never skate through pain. If something hurts, they need to get off the ice! This especially goes for hard hits to the head. When in doubt, sit them out. The rule should always be to play it safe. In a sport notorious for the toughness of its players, it can be especially difficult to get kids on board with this strategy. It can be helpful to educate your player about the injury or pain they're feeling and explain that focusing on healing will lead to a quicker return to having fun and playing the game at a higher level.

### Life Lessons Learned

With a broken wrist, my son, Joe, had to sit out gym class, but rather than send him to study hall, his physical education teacher at Christian Brothers Academy assigned him to research and write about his injury. While it didn't help his wrist heal any faster, it did help our sidelined hockey player understand why it was going to take some time to get back on the ice and work that wicked wrist shot again. It also didn't hurt his grades, as I seem to recall him scoring on A on this essay.

### My Wrist Fracture by Joey Burns, Age Twelve

This past October I suffered a very bad wrist fracture during a hockey game. As I discovered during my research, the injury, called a Salter Harris II, is very common among hockey players my age. We'll begin by explaining how I got hurt.

My peewee travel team was doing really well in the Columbus Weekend Tournament in Niagara Falls, New York. The first game we won 16-0! I was doing great with one goal and three assists. The next day we were all a bit tired and had a very early game. When the game started, I felt good and again my team was leading on the scoreboard. Toward the middle of the second period, we had two penalties, thus being down two men. The coaches sent me back out to "kill the penalty." Now, let me first tell you, checking is legal in hockey, which means you can knock down the player who has the puck to gain possession. I went behind the net to get the man who had the puck, and checked him. I got the puck and that's when my arm went into the boards straight on. My wrist snapped. I was in a lot of pain, but I kept on skating to kill off the penalty. I knew something was wrong, so I shot the puck to the other end and skated off the ice. When I got to the bench, everyone was patting my back because of the big "hit." Even the coach said, "That shook the boards!" Then I told him about the pain. They rushed me to the locker room where an on-staff EMT examined my wrist. When I pulled my glove off, I knew it was bad. The paramedic put a splint on my wrist and told my mom and dad we needed to go an emergency room for treatment. Instead of telling me that my wrist was broken, the EMT's words were "I want to be the first one to sign your cast." The rest of my day involved doctors, needles, meds, a cast, and a sharpie.

At the Buffalo Children's Hospital, I learned what type of injury I suffered and what my treatment would be. The doctor explained I had a Salter-Harris II, one of the most common fractures, and it was a fracture of my left radius. While it was common, the concern was the fact it was a growth plate fracture. The growth plate is an area of developing tissue and it is the weakest area of the growing skeleton. It is near the end of the long bones in children and it determines the future length and even the shape of the adult bone. As the doctor would explain, my fracture meant my bones had to be put back into place and immobilized for normal growth to continue. My injury did require X-rays to determine the fracture and decide on a treatment plan. The Buffalo doctor was an orthopedic pediatric surgeon, a doctor who specializes in bone and joint problems in children. He explained I would need to continue seeing an orthopedic surgeon in Syracuse.

After the X-Ray and diagnosis, the surgeon decided to reset the wrist. He began with long needles right where the break was and numbed the area. I still felt it when he snapped the wrist back in place. The pain was excruciating. Then he began with putting my effected limb in a full-arm cast. It went from my knuckle to above my elbow to limit any movement and prevent me from moving the radius. I was told to limit all physical activity. I had to apply ice for several days to reduce the swelling.

The wrist and hand are made up of twenty-seven bones and many ligaments, tendons, and muscles. There are eight carpal bones that serve as a link between forearm and hand and that allows for motion of the wrist. My hockey gear did not completely cover my wrist and hand area and therefore was exposed and vulnerable to injury. A study by the Mayo Clinic in Rochester on hockey injuries finds this to be a fairly common injury. Twenty-nine percent of the injuries observed during a hockey season for the study were fractures. The study observed injuries for my level of play, peewee, and observed four fractures, including two exactly like the kind I suffered. Interesting to note, the body sites most often injured were the shoulder and the arm. When a patient enters the emergency room with a broken wrist doctors have several options on how to treat the particular injury. They could put it in a cast, reset it, and surgically repair it (which is very rare), or even leave it to heal on its own. This all of course depends on the seriousness of the break, and the type of break.

Over time when you don't use certain muscles they deteriorate, this is called atrophy. Smell and dead skin will also start to form, as I now know all too well. Following is a picture of the actual X-Ray; this shows a fracture of my left radius. The break was right along the developing tissue. I have had three different casts: a full arm hard cast (put on first day), a short hard cast (put on three weeks after injury), and a short soft cast (made of an almost-rubber substance). The doctors explained normally he would keep someone in a hard cast for the entire time but since I was healing so well he felt I didn't need it. Through this entire experience everyone has been really great to me, my parents still being their corny selves, the doctors making jokes, and everyone else just seeing if I need help with anything. It has also made me very thankful for all the things I took advantage of being able to do before, like sports, video games, even eating with my left hand. All these things became difficult with the break and I am really thankful I will be able to do them again.

The kind side of people, I found really comes out when they saw me in a cast. They would immediately ask what happened and hoped I would feel better, and the best part was I could tell they meant every word. I have also gotten to see super heroes at work. No I don't mean superman or bat man, I mean true super heroes, doctors and Nurses giving hope and caring for those who really need them. I hope someday I can make that kind of difference in someone's life. Making them smile even in a hospital, that is what real heroes are like. I have also met a lot of nice people through all of this, whether they are doctors, nurses, coaches, or just kind strangers. This experience has also gave me hope—hope that people will still ask how I'm doing cast or no cast.

Now, of course, I am trying to prevent another injury and I found that staying fit, stretching, and wearing protective clothing greatly decreases the risk of injury. You must also avoid any physical contact when in pain because it could just result in a more severe injury. Always warm up before playing. In all sports, there is a risk of injury so if you are terribly afraid of being injured; maybe sports aren't the thing for you. When you do get injured you have to be extremely careful and remember you can't be aggressive you just have to take your time and let it heal. You have to have a certain mental toughness to prevent from just getting out there and playing. Although if you have a giant cast on your arm you're not going to be that tempted to play anyway. Hopefully people can learn from past mistakes and be more careful.

In hockey, as size increases so do injuries, which goes to show people need to be careful on what they are doing. Just because they're 6 foot 4, doesn't mean they have to play like an animal. I hope something has come out of reading this paper. Whether it is now you will be more careful next time, or you will just tip your hat to someone walking down the street, I just hope it puts things in perspective.

We try our darndest to prevent our kids from breaking bones, suffering sprains, and hitting their noggins. From investing in pads, helmets, and proper training . . . to yelling in the stands to keep their heads up! Prevention is always the best medicine, but injuries happen. When they do, don't lose your perspective.

Author's daughter Sophia, sidelined by a meniscus tear

## Here We Go Again

My tough little hockey girl has been hip-checked, tripped, whacked, and punched more than a few times during her hockey career that began at age three. She saw an earlier-than-expected end to her season with her 14U girls' team. But it wasn't hockey that sidelined her. There was an overlap in sports, with practice just getting started in lacrosse. A sudden stop and change in direction, and pop went the knee.

Sophia's injury was something our orthopedic surgeon hadn't seen in anyone so young. The very rare root tear of the medial meniscus (it actually had flipped 180 degrees) required an entirely different approach than a traditional meniscus surgery, and could not be repaired arthroscopically.

What was supposed to be an hour-and-a-half surgery was close to four with two surgeons. Six months off the ice, physical therapy, and a super positive attitude got her through it all. Thanks to her great doctors, Sophia returned to the ice with a renewed perspective on sports, increased motivation, and an increased ability to cope with season frustrations with a new mentally tough mindset.

Sophia ended up with fifteen staples down in her leg. Her response to that? "Fifteen? Wow, cool . . . that's my number!"

Her response when told by doctors she would have a scar? "Darn, does this mean my career as a leg model is over?"

# 36

## HOCKEY-INSPIRED POEM AND ESSAY

### Hockey Poem

My kids have been awarded all kinds of trophies, medals, and certificates for hockey. But the following are undoubtedly some of my greatest treasures. When my daughter was eight years old, she had to come up with a "funny" poem for her writing class. Her teacher would then submit the work as entries in a national contest. The challenge got Sophia to think about the reality and humor of being the only girl on her hockey team. They rhymes came easy to her. Among the thousands of entries, Sophia's won first place! She won a box of silly prizes and still hangs on to that annoying whoopee cushion. So the next time your hockey player gets stuck on a theme for a poem or essay, have them put down their sticks, pick up a pen, and think hockey!

## Hockey Girl with Guts

*By Sophia Burns, age eight*

I'm one of the few girls on my team
 And when the boys get mean
 I pull out my stick
 And skate real quick,
 My shot is really sick
 On the ice I'm never a bore,
 I love to score,
 I'm a puck hungry girl
 Who would rather shoot than twirl.

## Hockey Essay

Assigned by a teacher to come up with an example of how he defies convention, my son also chose a hockey theme for his essay. More proof hockey can awaken your kiddos' creative souls!

## Challenged and Inspired by Hockey

*By Joey Burns, age fourteen*

I defy convention through my work ethic, which developed and grew through my years of playing hockey. My generation has grown up expecting things to come to them instantly, in a snap! So much so that we have now been dubbed "generation now." Please don't lump me into that category. I'm the type of person who likes to work toward their goal, no matter how long it may take.

When I started playing hockey, at the age of eight, most of the kids around me were tremendously more advanced. They started skating as soon as they could walk. This certainly didn't give me the "edge" in this fast and furious sport. But instead of hanging up the skates, I was motivated to work even harder. I became determined to catch up to the kids who could literally skate circles around me and make the elite travel team. I dedicated an entire summer of my young life to hockey, practicing every day and shooting on the net in my driveway over and over again until my parents nagged me to come inside.

When I returned to the ice arena after that summer, the coaches saw a totally different skater. They were shocked to see the kid who struggled so much to keep up, now leading the pack. I tried out for the team that year and made it! That was one of the most satisfying feelings I have ever experienced, dedicating myself to a goal and then reaching it. Hockey provided a good life lesson for me. When I now set a goal for myself, I not only want to reach it, I want to exceed it and reach heights that I didn't even know were possible. That is how I defy convention in my life.

# 37

## ROCKIN' ROLES: KEY TO VOLUNTEERING IS FINDING A JOB THAT WORKS FOR YOU

**Wanted: Reliable parents** to work weekends in cold conditions. Must be organized, willing to answer phone calls during dinner, and keep the peace with dozens of well-meaning, opinionated hockey parents. No pay. Long hours.

Coaching positions shouldn't have to put out ads, but it seems every year fewer parents are willing or able to step up and pitch in for the team.

Given current economic conditions, many parents are working longer hours, or even holding two jobs, and many simply have less free time to spare.

But as my wise Italian mother would say after our big Sunday dinners, as we sat there with stuffed bellies, piled-up dishes, pots, and pans, "Many hands make light work." She would assign each of us a cleanup duty. Before we knew it, all six of us kids were out again playing before the sun settled for the night.

That same simple theory can help your coach run the team when parents provide valuable assists.

# 39

# DON'T BITE OFF MORE THAN YOU CAN CHEW

**S**o **who wants** to be a team manager?
I remember one season when the coach asked that question and all the parents lowered their heads. No hands went up. No one made eye contact. No surprise there. Who has the time and the energy for taking and making countless phone calls, booking teams, tournaments, organizing fundraisers, and dealing with other parents? It's challenging enough to get a decent meal in your kid's belly and get them to the rink on time with all their equipment.

Pile more duties onto an already full plate of just being a hockey parent? Run the risk of a mid-season meltdown? No, thank you.

In the excitement of a new season, and when no one else is volunteering, you might be tempted to find that inner hero and stick up your hand for every job. But Baldwinsville, New York, hockey mom Amy Colclough has some cautionary advice for those who get the urge to strap on the super hockey mom or dad cape.

"Remember that it's a long year, especially if you have other kids, and school/work will heat up, too," Colclough says. "If you don't think you'll enjoy the role, don't do it.

"Think about what you're really good at and stick to it. One mom was a photographer and she had her camera at every game. At season's end, she made a phenomenal book of photos for each player. Start with one job. You can always take on more."

If you do take on a leadership role, realize the job calls for diplomacy, says Carla Peacock, a hockey mom in Oswego, New York. She and her husband should know, having evolved from youth hockey coach and manager to college club hockey coach and manager.

"It is important that you don't come in like you know it all, and try to take over," Peacock says. "There are people who enjoy helping as much as you do."

Hummelstown, Pennsylvania, hockey mom Jen Kurzenknabe mastered the task of team manager by organizing and delegating.

"Being a hockey manager can be challenging, but once you have all the initial things done for your team like the meetings, paperwork, and volunteers, it is very rewarding to see all of your effort and planning put into action," she says.

Teams need parents to step up, and there's a job for everyone. Remember, just like your kid's team, it should be all for one and one for all.

## Team Manager Tips

*By Amy Colclough*

Before you commit, speak to coaches to find out what they expect from a team manager. You really have to understand how the head coach wants things done and be clear that the coaches must communicate with you.

### Game Scheduling and Tournaments

Some coaches want to do their own game scheduling. Game scheduling is like a second job.

Understand from coaches what levels and types of teams they want to play. How many tournaments would they like to do? How far do they want to travel?

### Parent Meetings and Communications

Who is doing what? Do you have a team Facebook page, everyone's email, phone numbers, etc.?

### Money Matters

How is it handled and on what level (organizationally) or do you need to get a team account set up? What are the parents feelings on fundraising? My last couple years as a hockey mom, parents wanted to write checks, not fundraise.

### Parent Assignments

Scorekeeping, clock, music, penalty boxes—set these expectations up front so everyone knows what is expected of them.

As a team manager, I always tried to make sure everything ran smoothly for the players—you want it to be a good life experience. Part of that is trying to keep parents happy by communicating with them. Looking back, the smoothest seasons started with a team outing of some sort, with parents, shortly after the team was picked. A cookout or potluck helps everyone get to know everyone.

Be aware of how far some players may have to travel for practices and games, and work with coaches to make this as easy as possible. When traveling to games and tournaments, consider looking at the area and if there are any fun things to do like a college game nearby, movies playing, or sights to see. Always send the address of the rink to people with the time their player must arrive ahead of each game. If you do fundraise, you really want the players to participate—it's their team after all. Ask them or give them options on what they might like to do. I had some fantastic, reliable parents that helped over the years. Keep it simple. Regarding delegating tasks—it depends on the parent group. Sometimes that works, sometimes it doesn't. In general, it seems less confusing for parents if communications came from one source. Managers who have happy hockey families did it for the team as a whole and not for their child only.

# 40

## HOCKEY MOM TAKES A PENALTY

### By Sharon Enck

**P**enalty box duty is right up there with fundraising, locker room duty, and for some, concession stand duty, as rites of passage for hockey parents. While we don't handle any of the concession stand stuff in our association (our local rinks take care of that), parents on my team do fundraise and we do spend our time in the penalty box.

Well, some of us.

For the past eight seasons I have successfully avoided this duty. As an inexperienced hockey mom, at first it seemed like only the dads would take over penalty box duty. I didn't see a lot of moms in there—moms were relegated to other assignments. I told myself that penalty box duty would take away from the experience of the game, that I wouldn't be able to focus on what was going on, and worse, that if the door didn't open right at that exact moment I needed it to, I would ruin everything. I would be mortified and surely the player, not to mention the coach, would be livid.

Turns out, I was wrong. On all counts.

As I've gone along, I've seen many a mom take a seat in the penalty box. Some even preferred it to other tasks, as it does impose some rules on you, ones that you wouldn't necessarily obey in the stands. Like the no talking rule, or in some parents' cases, the no shouting rule. One mom told me she needed to be in there so she wouldn't scream at her player, the refs, or the coach. *Wow.* As a parent, your only job in the penalty box is to just sit or stand there stoically and open/close the door when a penalty occurs. That's it. Maybe that's why I have avoided it for so long. Being quiet for an entire hour? Not my strong suit.

However, as a hockey mom and as a hockey-mom blogger, I felt I could no longer shirk the experience. So, I went for the gusto by asking to be put in there during playoffs. It's all or nothing for me.

So, one Saturday morning I got all geared up in my heavy jeans, boots, big coat, scarf, warm hat, and mittens. Did I mention that we were playing an early morning game in the coldest rink in town? I had been warned that the box is much colder than the stands, so I went prepared.

I took my position in the box and said a shy "good morning" to the scorekeeper, who probably identified me as a newbie right away, but thankfully kept his opinions to himself. Watching the warm-ups, I thought it couldn't hurt to take a few pictures right? I run the social media for my kids' team and it's my responsibility to report on the game.

*Click, click.*

No one noticed, and if they did they didn't care, so I got a little more brazen and filmed a video. Then the impossible happened, I relaxed. Despite the waves of nauseating hockey stink that came from our bench through the cracks in the glass, it was fun to just sit there. I felt like I was more a part of the game than I ever had been. I heard the coach's instructions, chatter from the players, and their heavy breathing from a tough shift. Also, I wasn't distracted by my fellow parents in the stands. I was 100 percent focused on each play.

It was way more exciting than being in the stands, and when my first "customer" came in? It went off without a hitch. I didn't forget to open the door at the right time, the door didn't jam as I had feared, and the player and I didn't once collide during the event.

The player even let me take a selfie with her at the end. (Thanks Captain Audrey!) Pretty sure I broke a rule there, though.

There are plenty of ways hockey families can cut costs. "Stretching Your Budget."
*Credit:* Darren Gygi

# 41

## STRETCHING YOUR HOCKEY BUDGET DURING THE SEASON

**A**s wise hockey moms, we clip coupons, scour ads, comparison shop, and readily succumb to the lure of BOGO (buy-one, get-one) to keep the hockey family budget skating along a smooth sheet of ice. But regardless, hockey is an expensive sport and budgets are bound to get hip-checked into the boards from time to time. League fees, travel expenses, and equipment costs can rip through your wallet faster than a Joe Sakic wrister.

With that in mind, some hockey parents have been kind enough to share some sage advice to help you keep the fun up and the costs down:

- Shop, swap, and save. Remember the player makes the equipment; the equipment doesn't make the player. Never refuse hand-me-downs, but never skimp on the helmet. —*Jessica Lynn, Cicero, New York*

- Trade equipment with fellow parents. It seems if you have one kid in hockey, the others follow suit. —*Kenyetta Reese, Batavia, New York*

- Look for last year's equipment models. You can save money when your local hockey shop clears out inventory, or even get a deal on equipment that was special-ordered for a customer who changed their mind. Also, locate your local shoe repair shop. They can repair skate boots and protective pads, even goalie pads. —*Diane Pelton, Camillus, New York*

- Seek sponsors and raise funds. My kids play for a fully sponsored team: Ed Snider Youth Hockey. The sponsor and the youth hockey organization covers everything including equipment and USA Hockey registration. —*Kristie Wisniewski, Philadelphia, Pennsylvania*

- Our kids collected returnable bottles and cans to raise money for goody bags for the end of games (avoiding fast food) and a tournament DVD. —*Cecilia Jennifer, Cicero, New York*

- Share a ride to the rink. If you're along for the ride, offer to chip in for gas or pay for a meal. —*Cathy Tanzella, Camillus, New York*

- Drive by the drive-thrus. My family packs a snack/drink bag for each game. The snacks are for my hockey player after the game and his sister during the game. Our own snacks are more healthful and way cheaper. —*Stephanie Schlott Folsom, Manchester, New Hampshire*

- We used an old hockey bag to bring a small microwave, griddle, and utensils to hotels. Grilled cheese and soup make good snacks between games. Hotel honor system members can earn points towards a free stay and late check-outs after championship games. —*Pam Munson, Syracuse, New York*

- For long days and weekends on the road, bring along your Crock-Pot and blender. There's nothing better than pulled chicken sandwiches and your own healthful protein smoothies for the team to enjoy in between games. —*Kim Marie Buske Shepard, Oswego, New York*

- I save money on sticks by getting leftover sticks from a local junior team at the end of the season. They are all new sticks that normally sell for between $275 to $300 and I buy last year's models to stock up about half price. The junior teams get the sticks in bulk at the beginning of the season and want to get rid of the extras at the end of the season. Great deals to be had! —*Micheal Farnham, Minneapolis, Minnesota*

- Cross my fingers and hope the bank manager doesn't notice! But, seriously, I try and buy used but in good condition where I can, and if it's something new (especially something like a mask) make it a Christmas or birthday present. And yes, I have a goalie, so the cost of it is a similar size to the national debt of a small country, especially when he's having a growth spurt! We also have to travel by boat and bus to all of our away games, but the club does spread the cost across the home games, which helps a lot with budgeting! —*Linda Aitcheson, Belfast, United Kingdom*

- Staying in hotel bringing your own food, even microwave. Beats paying for every meal. In different places find free things to do between games especially if you have other children that don't play hockey. As far as equipment my goalie never would wear used equipment, there is hope as he now pays for his own. —*Suzanne Wolff-Kozikoski, Liverpool, New York*

- My son has lots of chores but doesn't get paid in money. He knows that because he plays hockey, I can't afford a cleaning service, lawn service, or pool person. He earns hockey. —*Julie Bennett, Fulton, New York*

- Virtual garage sales, consignment shops, and eBay are all resources that I use readily to sell old gear. Most of my son's hockey equipment is already used, so used sporting goods stores don't always take them. We have friends in Canada who travel back and forth frequently, so for most of my son's new items, such as skates and sticks, our friends purchase them in Canada and bring them here. So much cheaper! Also, if you can convince your coach to go to a tournament during Boxing Week in Canada, you can find some amazing deals. —*Robin Johnson, Virgilio, Illinois*

- Don't wait until the last minute to go looking. If your state has any tax-free shipping days, then buy your priced items then, if you can. Shop around and do some online searches. My son has tried on lots of equipment at the store, and we've found it cheaper online. Also, some teams do swap meets on used equipment. Used doesn't mean old. That's the other fight I have with my son and his gear sometimes. —*Johnny Sheppard, Scarborough, Maine*

- Secondhand shops like Play It Again Sports are my best friends! We also bring Crock-Pots, sandwiches, and other food whenever possible (some rinks frown upon that practice). At the hotel, we try to reserve a banquet room for a team dinner. —*Chris High, Pittsburgh, Pennsylvania*

- We do team meals where we all bring one item from a team list. Find the other parent who is traveling without the rest of the family and split a room. Get a bunch of plastic bins and start an equipment donation program for your organization. Clearance or last year's model is the only way to buy any type of equipment. —*Gregory Paro, Rochester, New York*

- We research equipment/sizes at local stores then search online to see if we can find a better deal. We saved almost $100 over local prices on the last growth spurt. Also, if you buy online, you may want to check out ebates.com. They pay you a small percentage of what you spend. —*Tammy Thomas Myers, Oswego, New York*

- Go large, it's hockey season! —*Mark Donabella, Oswego, New York*

- Just hope you get a work bonus and a tax return. —*Jeremy Grosdidler, Mitchell, South Dakota*

- We pack our food, do Crock-Pot and Instant Pot meals between a few families so we never have to eat out while travelling. —*Dawn Miranda, Cranbrook, British Columbia*

Lastly, give your gently used gear to another family and pass along your money-saving experiences to help their budgets shoot and score, too.

# 42

## THE PEAKS AND PITFALLS OF FUNDRAISING

---

**B**ig on dreams. Short on cash. Isn't that the case every hockey season? The challenge is to find fundraisers that are big on cash and short on stress. Easier said than done.

The season is stressful enough you certainly don't want to be the source of Duck-and-cover syndrome, where family and friends see you coming and yell, "Duck everyone, and cover your wallet."

When my son landed a spot on a travel team, I was thrilled. I figured it meant more travel and more games. But I had no clue it also meant more dollars. The blow was softened when the coaches explained we would not have to shoulder all the costs for travel and tournaments.

Then they said it, the dreaded "F" word. Fundraising. Nooooo!

At that point in my life, I had my fill of fundraising, and so had those around me. Friends would point at me and warn others, "Look out, here comes Christie Wonka and her Fundraising Factory." Chocolate bars, cookie dough, holiday wreaths, water bottles, pies, candles, iPod raffles, stadium seats, jewelry—I've hawked it all.

That year, our team decided to hit the neighborhoods for a bottle-and-can drive as our main fundraising effort. It took a lot of effort, but we gained more than money that day. We watched in amazement as our young hockey players tackled this task like a team determined to win a championship game. They divided and conquered neighborhoods, scooping up cans and dropping them into the back of our pickup trucks with the speed and precision of a well-executed breakout.

By the end of our drive we were exhausted, sticky, and smelly. That day we collected more than seven thousand bottles and cans and a nifty $420 profit. Plus, the kids got to know each other outside of their pads and practices. Parents found common ground, too. That's a huge plus when you can develop that kind of bonding early on, before the start of a long season.

So the next time someone on your kid's team drops the "F word" on you, think about the other benefits that surface when you work together as a team to achieve a common goal.

## Organize a Bottle-and-Can Drive
### Promote
Send out flyers with information about your drive and a phone number for people to call and offer to drop cans off at your redemption center.

### Pick a Time
Timing is everything. Our team leader picked the Sunday after Thanksgiving for our drive. It worked out well, as neighbors were eager to rid their garages of emptied containers after Thanksgiving feasts, and they were in a generous spirit as well.

### *Divide and Conquer*

Put your kids in different age groups or different positions so they get to know other players. Show your colors by wearing your team jersey or t-shirts with a team logo; it legitimizes the operation and reinforces the team concept for the kids. Representative coaches and parents should speak about safety and good manners.

### *Redeem*

Find a kind and willing redemption center that will let you set up an account for your team for year-round donations.

# 43

# TURN YOUR TEAM AROUND: GET THE NUMBERS UP!

**I**s your youth hockey program battling to reverse a downturn in participation? We're here to help. Behind every good fighter is a good trainer. In your corner is skilled and seasoned hockey mom Kristin Fleet Haag, CPA Treasurer with the Rome Youth Hockey Association. Rome's program has seen a remarkable turnaround in recent years, thanks to a strategy of working as a team.

## How to Grow the Game

*By Kristin Fleet Haag*

We are located in Rome, New York, a community that has seen a declining population and a changing demographic over the last twenty-five years. In 1985, we were a huge hockey town, where both high school teams were Section 3 Champs and New York State Champs for both Division I and Division II High School Hockey. We now have only one high school in our community.

In 2008–09, despite our city completing a $3 million renovation on our hockey facility, the Bill Fleet Rink at the John F. Kennedy Civic Arena saw little action. Shortly after that our participation numbers declined pretty drastically.

Our learn-to-skate or initiation program numbers decreased from over a hundred skaters to just sixty skaters in a few short years. Of course, that is the feeder program to our higher levels. We knew we had to take action.

I joined the board in 2012, when my son, who was going to be a second-year peewee, was not going to have a travel team to play on. By the time the season actually rolled around, there was no house team either. Additionally, my youngest son had just started in the learn-to-skate program. At that point, I knew I needed to do something and joined the board. My dad, who is a lifetime member, also was actively involved. We held meetings with community members and hockey folks to brain storm how to get our numbers up.

### *Keys to Victory*

We hired a marketing firm and launched a print and media campaign. It was relatively expensive, but well worth the investment. Our initial participation numbers grew back to over a hundred that year. We continue to run the campaign each year. We used our hometown NHL/AHL Stars Tim and Tom Sestito in the commercials for us.

We also worked with the city of Rome to reduce our ice fees. My first year, I negotiated a temporary reduction. The second year, I negotiated a permanent reduction. We went from an average of $105 per hour to $85 per hour. When our ice fees were lower, we were able lower our registration fees and increase volume.

We sold ourselves to the community. We started attending community events and we made our ice slots more working-parent friendly. Some teams used to practice at 6:00 a.m. before school. We rearranged the ice slots so that all practices started after 5:00 p.m.

My second year, we wanted a better handle on our numbers, so we offered an early registration discount at 25 to 30 percent savings. My third year, we reduced that cost even further. We are now arguably the lowest price shop in town. Squirt and up are at $425, mites at $215, and learn-to-skate at $160. This year we launched our online registration process.

For tournaments, we invested time and sweat equity. My first year, there was no mite tournament. In 2015, we hosted a mite tournament with eighteen teams and the following year we had twenty-six teams with over 310 kids.

We rebranded ourselves, by changing our colors, logo, and jerseys, without charging our members. One of our board members wrote a grant securing $22,000 for the purchase of new jerseys.

In 2017 we purchased cross-ice dividers, partnering with the city of Rome. Also, we applied and secured a grant for USA Hockey's Grow the Game Grant.

We are a 501C3 organization, which is pretty important when looking to secure grant funding.

Best of luck to you and your organization!

# 44

# PROS AND CONS
# OF USED EQUIPMENT

**When is it** safe to scrimp and when should you cough up the cash to buy brand-new equipment?

This debate among my Facebook friends began with Skaneateles, New York, hockey mom Alyssa Tauber Militello. Her response? "Pro: cost. Con: the stink of a stranger." You make a pungent point, Alyssa. Stink can sink any savings.

There's nothing cheap about hockey, and your wallet can take a hit when your kids are growing like weeds. Who can blame a parent for wanting to buy used? But, buyer beware. I teamed up with Pittsburgh's Dana Vento for some factors to consider.

Our top concern is always safety. Helmets, chest protectors, gloves, and face masks are all pieces that are best bought new because materials like padding, foam, and straps can wear out over time and fail to protect our kids. As padding is used over and over, it hardens and weakens.

Did you know face masks and helmets have safety guidelines prescribed by the Hockey Equipment Certification Counsel (HECC)? Avoid buying used because it's tough to tell just how used the equipment is. Gloves have critical padding, which can withstand the hit of hockey sticks, pucks, and skates. Holes in gloves, or worn-down padding on the outer part of the hand, can lead to serious injuries.

Be sure to check the shells of used skates. They have to be in great shape for all those hits.

At garage sales, the price may look right, but consider what you don't know. How long has the gear been in an attic, garage, or shed? How much sun, heat, or playing time has the equipment been exposed to?

There are some pieces of equipment you can purchase without worry, including hockey socks, elbow pads, knee pads (without cracks), sticks, and pants with no rips, tears, or missing padding. For mite-aged players who see less action, it's probably more of a score to buy used.

But always carefully inspect the gear. As Vento points out, "When buying used, you can never be too careful."

You may save a few bucks, but consider what it could end up costing. If your player is not protected, there are no second chances.

# 45

## SECONDHAND SAVES: HOCKEY GEAR SWAP

**While my daughter** is always looking to upgrade her hockey gear, I'm looking for ways to swap and save. One player's gently used shin and elbow pads are this mom's treasure. Good gear, already broken in, and super cheap? I'm all in!

More hockey organizations are recognizing the dent hockey can put on the family budget and are offering an assist in the form of gear swap meets. Families can find great deals on gear for the upcoming season while getting rid of equipment their kids have outgrown.

Julie Bennett, a hockey mom in Fulton, New York, holds a sale on the same day as registration at the rink through her hockey organization. "We were able to help new parents with what their child would need and make sure the equipment fit the kids correctly," Bennett says. "This was also a great way for new parents and players to meet other hockey parents. Let's face it, it's nice to see a familiar face when you are new to a sport and may not know anyone."

Bennett advises parents to bring their kids with them to take the guesswork out of properly fitting them.

Inventory tracking and good old-fashioned organizational skills have been the keys to successful equipment swaps for the Huskies Hockey Club in Romeoville, Illinois, a southwest suburb of Chicago. Organizer Nikki Ommen times it for the end of summer and before the fall tryouts.

"This way people were already in the building, no special trips are needed to the rink if some live farther away," says Ommen.

She also suggests starting gear collection early and in advance of the sale, so it can be put in an inventory, but not too far in advance to avoid storing it for a long period of time.

Ommen's equipment sale is also tied into club fees. If you donated items to sell, 100 percent of the sold price goes directly to your hockey fees for the upcoming season. That makes fees more affordable and gets gently used gear out of the house.

Another tip from Ommen for organization's planning a gear swap is to spread the word. Go big on advertising and see your savings grow too!

## More Tips from Nikki and Julie
### Swap before the Season

Avoid additional trips to find gear. Hosting a swap meet at the rink during a registration event gives parents a chance to sign up the kids and also browse and buy gear. Collect the gear in advance and create an inventory, but time it so you don't have to store it for a long period of time.

### The "Save-on-Fees" Option

Tie equipment sales to club fees. If you donate items to sell, 100 percent of the sold price goes directly to your hockey fees for the upcoming season. This allows families to pay down fees and get gently used gear out of the house.

### In the Bag

Have plastic bags handy so people can carry their items home with ease. Organize gear in groups by using signage and post flyers to help families find where they need to go.

### Leftovers for Charity

Living in the Chicago suburbs, there are many not-for-profit hockey organizations that always need help. For families who didn't want their items back, we donated the remaining pieces of gear to one or more of the organizations. Contact your local NHL team for leads on who to contact in order to donate gear.

# 46

## ORGANIZING YOUR HOCKEY HOUSEHOLD

**F**ew of us ever gracefully glide into the challenging role of a hockey parent. It's more like a face plant. Or a belly flop. Once you've learned the quickest way to the rink, how to dress your kid, and the difference between icing and offsides, there are still a ton of things to figure out.

### Advice from the Experts

I was fortunate enough to receive great advice from other hockey moms; and now it's time for me to pay it forward.

### *There's an App for That*

Jodi Lupo, a hockey mom from Baldwinsville, New York, is a big fan of the Cozi Family Organizer. It color-codes, sends reminder texts, and links her entire family into one calendar. When she and her husband make changes, it updates everyone who needs to know. Her kids can log on from a laptop to see what's on the horizon.

## *What to Do with Stinky Hockey Bags*

If the idea of sifting through the moldy mysteries of a hockey bag disgusts you, you may want to follow the lead of hockey mom Teri Parks. After each game and practice, the rule is to pull out and hang up the gear. Her squirt daughter, Maddie, and mite son, Gavin, have a designated drying area for their equipment. Parks prefers to have the hockey bags hang too.

"Any strong hook or two should be able to hold the bag or you can use a coat rack," Parks suggests.

Keeping things vertical saves precious space. Stick wall mounts are great too, especially when you place them on a wall where the sticks are easy to grab and go.

## *Know Where to Find Hockey Clothes*

Keeping hockey clothing separate from regular clothing can score you some points in the staying organized department. For Trenna Brodey Kelley, from Weatherford, Texas, that means a separate dresser drawer for her son Zander's jerseys, socks, and Under Armour.

And to share the joy of hockey, Ann Schneid, from Baldwinsville, New York, donates outgrown skates and gently used sticks and gear to community programs for low-income families.

"Hockey is a wonderful sport that should be experienced by all children," she says.

## Hockey Decluttering Checklist

But we're just getting started. Syracuse Nationals Hockey mom Teri Parks, owner of Teri Parks Design Appeal Home Staging, put together this game plan to get organized!

## *The Equipment*

Biggest complaint as a hockey parent is where to put all that (stinky!) hockey equipment. Well, unless you have your own locker room in your home, this is sometimes challenging. A whole book can be written on how to avoid smelly hockey equipment and skates. But, the first task to tackle in organizing your hockey household is to have an equipment "drying area." This can be a section of the basement, mudroom, or part of the laundry room as long as there is air circulating and it's at room temperature. It's important for you to dry equipment in a warm room as it will dry faster and there is less chance for bacteria to grow. There are many cheap drying racks available that you can hang equipment on between uses. Or you can even make your own using hockey sticks. If the only space you have available is in the garage, I would suggest a "hockey locker" or cabinet that contains a heat drying system (you can find these pretty reasonably priced online). A hockey cabinet not only serves a purpose of drying the equipment, but also acts as a place of storage, so visually it makes things look neater in your space.

## *The Bag*

The hockey bag's purpose is to transport the equipment, not to keep hockey equipment inside for hours and hours. After each game/practice, the equipment should be taken out of the bag and hung up to dry as mentioned above. Once you've designated an area of your house as the "drying area" for equipment, there also needs to be a place to hang/put the hockey bag other than the floor. Any strong wall hook (may need two) can hold a hockey bag or you can use a coat rack, especially if you have more than one to keep things vertical, which uses less space.

## *The Skates*

Hockey skates are not cheap and should also be cared for properly and stored in their own designated place. An inexpensive tip to drying skates faster is to place them on your register heaters or the use of drying racks will also do the trick. Once dry, skates can be stored away in decorative bins on shelving unit next to equipment. Be sure to use blade covers on skates when putting in bins. Or you can mount metal skate organizing racks to wall.

## *The Sticks*

There are several ways you can store hockey sticks. There are many varieties of stick wall mounts available. Be sure to place them on a wall where it would be easy to just grab and go. If you have a hockey equipment cabinet, you can mount two single hockey stick holders on each side giving you a spot to place four sticks. If your hockey equipment area is in the basement and you have lower hanging ceilings, you can make your own overhanging hockey stick holder by using two pieces of $4 \times 4$ about six to seven feet long, screw in four heavy-duty screw hooks (two on each end of $4 \times 4$), hang steel linked chain (length depends on how low you want holder to hang down from ceiling) pieces on each of the four screw hooks and mount to ceiling. Once holder is up, place hockey sticks alongside the $4 \times 4$s. They can hold up to twenty sticks!

## *The Jerseys*

You can use a simple portable clothes rack with hangers for hockey jerseys that is in the open for drying purposes or once jersey is dry, place in a closet/cabinet that would be near the rest of the equipment.

## *The Space*

Another suggestion in keeping your hockey area neat and presentable is to use a corner of a wall (ex: basement or garage) and build out a 5-inch-wide × 2-to 3-inch-deep area using two wood or metal rods from one wall to the other near the ceiling where you can hang a curtain. This way everything is contained and organized in one concealed spot, air is able to circulate for drying purposes, and it would be decoratively appealing.

When organizing your hockey space, you need to keep in mind space that will be functional for drying, big enough to keep all hockey items together (you don't want your equipment in the basement, hockey sticks in the garage, and skates in the mudroom), and as decoratively appealing as possible!

# 47

## WHEN HOCKEY IS NOT A FAMILY AFFAIR

**A**s soon as my daughter could walk, she wanted to skate. She had been to every one of her brother's hockey games, sometimes with her nose pressed up against the Plexiglas, clapping and yelling as soon as he stepped onto the ice.

She couldn't wait for it to be her turn. It didn't take long for her wobbly little penguin-like struts to turn into quick, confident strides. She suited up at the tender age of three as a mini-mite and thirteen years later is still going strong, chasing a puck around with her hands firmly planted on a stick. We became one united happy, hockey family.

Still, I often wonder how other hockey parents strike that happiness balance with their children who don't play hockey. Sometimes affectionately called the rink rats, you spot them running around the arena, or begrudgingly tagging along, forced to watch a sister or brother on the ice, when they openly admit they would rather be anywhere else.

Onondaga, New York, hockey dad and coach Marty Sicilia admits it's not easy, but he and his wife make every effort to give each of their children's interests an equal amount of attention. His daughter is a goalie. His son is an actor, singer, and dancer. Marty grew up as a jock and his comfort zone is an ice rink. His son's theatrical world is foreign to him, but he takes the time to learn.

"It's been eye opening for me and really pretty cool," he says. "I've been to the New York City ballet. Who could have imagined? As long as my kids are happy and healthy, I have nothing to complain about."

Sports has posed many challenges to the Coggiola family too. Jill Coggiola and her husband John, a coach for a Lysander, New York, hockey team, have been through the process of bringing along their three kids to events for many years with t-ball, baseball, and softball starting at age four, and then later with the addition of hockey.

"We also spend a lot of time at musical events as all our kids are equally involved in numerous ensembles as well," Coggiola says. "We approach all of these things as a family event. When our kids were younger that might have meant that we packed along a lot of snacks and books, a few extra balls and gloves, or in the case of hockey, a stick or two, and a few balls. The kids learned to become comfortable in the different environments (be it a quiet concert hall, any number of baseball/softball fields, or the various rinks we've been to around the state). They learn what they should and shouldn't do depending on the venue and event. These are life skills that they'll take with them forever."

Other hockey parents use instant gratification tactics to keep a kid from feeling tortured during tournaments and having meltdowns in rinks. They might buy them a new toy or head to the nearest mall during an out-of-town trip.

But while that may keep the whining down, licensed psychologist Tanya Gesek cautions parents not to go too far to try to make things equal and give in too much to "make their kids happy."

"Fair is never really equal," Gesek says. "Learning that lesson early is not a bad thing. Sibling rivalry can be healthy in moderation and helps kids develop important coping skills to manage frustration and challenges as an adult. It is more than OK to allow our kids to deal with not being happy and a little bored once in a while without a lot of 'stuff' or instant entertainment. In order to manage uncomfortable feelings, we have to feel them occasionally."

Parents may end up feeling the pain, but these growing pains are all a part of raising good kids who learn how to respect each other and each other's interests.

Being a coach and parent has its challeges. *Credit:* Darren Gygi

# 48

## STRIKING A BALANCE BETWEEN COACH AND PARENT

---

**E**ven the most hardened sports fan can admit to getting a little choked up when *Field of Dreams* hits its crescendo as Kevin Costner's character asks, "Hey, Dad . . . you wanna have a catch?"

Such is the power of sports when it comes to creating a powerful, emotional bridge between parent and child that extends beyond the field of play.

But what happens when the lifeline as a parent intersects that of coach? Even the best parent-child relationship can be strained when mom or dad grabs a clipboard and a whistle.

Lancaster, Pennsylvania, hockey dad Tim Frey knew there would be more than a few rough patches when he signed on to coach his son's peewee team. His biggest challenge was making sure he didn't "over-coach" his young goalie, especially away from the rink. That's why he had one of his assistants serve as his son's position coach.

"I was hoping that hearing advice from a different voice, it might register better than if Dad was giving the same suggestions," Frey says.

Sometimes coaches are guilty of overcompensating when it comes to talking with their son or daughter about their performance. It can be a struggle to be a fair coach to your own child. Leave discipline and criticism at the rink and talk about other things on the ride home.

"I am quite often much harder on my own child as I expect a very high level of respect and sportsmanship," says Dave Harter from Camillus, New York.

Coach Nathan Brightbill advises, "Praise them when they deserve it, instead of being worried the team parents think you're showing favoritism."

It's all a matter of striking that balance between coach—who wants what's best for the team—and parent—who wants what's best for his or her child. Do that, and you'll cultivate the trust of everyone on the team—including your son or daughter—and create memories that will last a lifetime.

"I relish the time he and I get to spend together heading to the rinks," Frey says.

"The greatest joy I got to experience as a coach was being able to place a medal around my son's neck after winning our league championship, or tapping him on the mask when heading to the handshake line."

Juggling school and hockey is a balancing act. *Credit:* Darren Gygi

# 49

## CRACKING DOWN TO MAKE SURE THEY CRACK THE BOOKS

**A**s any great coach knows, you don't necessarily coach each and every player the same way. Perhaps one kid responds to being challenged. Make getting higher grades a competition, just like scoring goals or earning a spot in the starting lineup.

Another kid needs hard parameters set—no grades, no games.

For our daughter, high school hockey requires practice every day after school in a rink that is forty minutes away, followed by weight training or yoga. There are days when she's so whipped after practice that she wants to call it a night. But if she wants to keep lacing up the skates, she's got to keep those grades up, too.

Fond du Lac, Wisconsin, hockey dad Peter Bellendir's son plays for a team that puts them on the road for more than an hour each way to the rink. But before committing to the team they made a deal that their son had to maintain no less than a B average, thus putting grades before hockey.

Minneapolis hockey dad Michael Farnham's son has heard a similar lecture. "He understands this and knows if his grades slip there's no hockey," Farnham says. "He has learned to schedule time to get his work done and he's doing a great job at it."

Sometimes "it" takes a little extra prodding on the part of parents.

"We travel with our sixteen-year-old daughter a lot," says Danbury, Connecticut, mom Anne Michelle Tonic. "We find that we have to stay on her. She can be lazy, unless it's hockey."

Tonic's daughter could barely skate five years ago and is now one of the fiercest defensemen on her team.

Hockey has shown how determination can be channeled and applied to other areas of life like school work.

Bill Colclough suggests that teammates offer themselves up as tutors for those who may need a little extra help. "My son would arrive early at practice to help out a teammate having trouble in physics," says the Baldwinsville hockey dad. "You may even be able to help them in a subject that they're having trouble with."

Skaneateles, New York, parents Jeff and Julie Torrey found an important key to success: structure and clear expectations. Their kids have learned to prioritize schoolwork so it doesn't become overwhelming with their hectic schedules.

"They know that homework needs to get done before that evening's practice," Julie says. "The most challenging aspect of the balancing act would be helping our kids realize that proper rest and not getting run down is essential to both school and hockey success."

It gets more challenging as they get older. That's why Monarchs Tier 1 girls' team coaches Tosh Farrell and Dave Broussard, from Rochester, New York, say when it's time to talk time management with your teen, the word sacrifice needs to be part of the conversation.

One thing is certain, says Farrell—no matter how skilled or talented a player is, if he/she does not become competent in time management, their chances of becoming a college athlete drop dramatically. Even if college athletics is not on your radar, honing your time management skills will greatly increase the likelihood of success in college and beyond.

Broussard, a high school health teacher, advises parents to help their child formulate a schedule that accommodates all aspects of their busy, active lifestyle. "Those organizational and time management skills are imperative in college life," says Broussard. "Especially when there is no parent around to aid and guide the student all of the time."

"It takes a lot of discipline to excel both on the ice and in the classroom. A good student that is also a proven competitor gives the athlete a leg up in the real world," says Tosh.

In a nutshell, parenting is serving as your child's coach in life. And just like any great phenomenon can attest, you don't scale life's mountains without guidance. Or a little tough love.

# 50

## HOW TO MOTIVATE WITHOUT GOING OVERBOARD

**Normally when a** baseball coach makes a trip to the mound during a pressure situation, there's not much fanfare. Perhaps he is just trying to buy some time, or talk over some strategy.

When a "mound visit" flashed across my computer screen in the form of a viral video, I had to stop and pay attention. In this particular instance, the coach told his pitcher he loved him, then added a, "Hey! Cheer up! Have some fun."

This particular instance took place during the Little League World Series, and you couldn't help but feel the strings of your heart being pulled in eight different directions as a father reminded us all why we do what we do as parents.

As it turns out, you don't need a magical cornfield in Iowa to understand that sports can bond parent and child, while also creating lifelong memories and lessons.

But how best to teach those lessons?

Do we financially incentivize our kids, bribing them with scenarios like, score a hat trick and get a new stick? Those types of deals don't exactly scream teamwork, selflessness, and sacrifice.

For Kevin Ahern, Syracuse National AAA girls hockey coach, it's always dad first and coach second.

"It's not about what I say. Rather, it's about creating experiences that have the potential to motivate," Ahern says.

Those positive experiences might include a trip to a local pro game, locker room visits, or attending a camp at a college. As tempting as it may be, Ahern strongly advises parents to steer clear of car coaching. "It's so dangerous," he says. "We dwell on all the negatives, and that is what is in our young athlete's mind that they will equate with their performance, some to the point of not wanting to play anymore."

Even if it kills him, Ahern picks out the positives of his daughters' games and then days later on the way to practice, may slip in a few things to work on.

For Ahern's wife, Darcy, it's important to leave lines of communication open for any type of conversation or venting, and she's careful not to fuel any fires.

"We don't talk about what others are doing. We focus on them and what they have within their power to improve or change," she says. "Motivation has to come from within the player, not the parent."

Kids are motivated by learning and having fun. Things can get pretty mucked up with expectations, politics, and external pressure—all adult themes. So when in doubt, just let the kids enjoy play, and enjoy the game. They have plenty of time to grow up.

# 51

## THE NUMBER ONE TRAIT OF A GREAT SPORTS PARENT IS . . .

### By Kevin Duy

**I**f you're competitive and passionate about helping your child succeed, it's easy to get carried away when it comes to youth sports. Games can get exciting. There can be pressures to put your kid into more training, personal coaching, and year-round leagues.

Unless you're conscious about making sure things don't get out of hand, they will get out of hand. Including your own emotions.

In my humble opinion, the number one trait of a great sports parent is . . . perspective.

When you have perspective, it's difficult to allow your emotions and competitiveness get the best of you. Perspective can keep you from getting wrapped up in the craziness, stress, and politics found in many youth sports organizations today.

### Four Key Areas Where Perspective Goes a Long Way

1. Time: These years of youth sports go by so fast. Before you know it, your child will be grown and you'll miss

the chaotic schedules, games, and even practices. I've found myself thinking things like, "I can't wait until he's older and can [fill in the blank]." They'll be older soon enough. Embrace, soak in, and capture the moments you have with them right now. You never know. They may decide to stop playing before they ever reach the point in time you've been so busy looking forward to. Then you'll look back are realized all the great moments you took for granted.

2. Referees and Umpires: I know, I know. It can be difficult to find really good officials. And it can be frustrating when a bad call goes against your kid. This is where perspective is so important. Game officials are just regular people who enjoy sports like you and me. Refereeing your kid's soccer game on a Saturday afternoon is taking them away from their own family. It's not their full-time profession. They're there to earn some extra money. They don't have it out for your kid's team. They're human and don't have instant replay. They're doing the best that they can. Do you think they want to blow a call so that they have to deal with other grown adults yelling at them and disrespecting them? And here's the biggest point about referees and umpires: kids can't play real games without them.

3. Coaches: Unless a coach is disrespectful to the kids and parents, does something to embarrass your team and organization, or puts kids in harm's way, we should think long and hard before criticizing him or her. When was the last time your child played for a coach who was paid to coach? My point is, youth sports coaches are volunteers.

They don't have to take on that responsibility, but they do. And they do it to help your kid. There's a lot of stress involved with being a coach and being second guessed by parents is a recipe for disaster. The best thing you can give a coach is your support, cooperation, respect, and of course, proper perspective.

4. Big Picture: Even though this one is labeled number four, I actually believe it's the most important one. So many sports parents become borderline obsessed with their child being the best player on their team, in their league, and in their city. They're constantly pushing and pressuring their kid to succeed. I get stressed out just by observing some of these parents. Imagine how their kids feel! It's difficult enough to succeed in sports. No kid needs added pressure from his own parents. Who cares if your kid is the best hockey player in the league when he's ten years old if he burns out by age fourteen and is a complete jerkface by twenty?

In the grand scheme of things, the most important outcome from youth sports is how they help your child develop into an awesome adult. If used properly, sports can help your child become an adult with tremendous leadership skills, great work ethic, sound communication skills, empathy, integrity, determination, class, the ability to embrace failure and learn from it, and enjoy victory without gloating.

When your child is an adult, hopefully he or she will be able to look back upon his or her youth sports days with fond memories and positive feelings. These things are way more important than the outcome of any game. In fifteen to twenty years, the games won't matter, but who your child became and what your relationship is like as a result of it all will mean more than anything.

That's perspective.

It may take more than a nudge when a player is the new kid on the team. *Credit:* Darren Gygi

# 52

# THE NEW KID ON THE TEAM

**My daughter is,** like most athletes, a fiercely loyal kid who likes familiarity. So you can imagine how the conversation went when we told her it was time to switch to a girls' team. From the mouth of my tough little hockey player came a resounding, "No way!"

I knew it wasn't going to be an easy sell. The boys on her team were like brothers. She'd been suiting up in black and purple since the age of three. These are the teammates who fist-bumped her after goals and shared the glorious moment of being handed a first-place trophy. The wins, the losses, the knee-hockey battles in the hotel hallways, and those big tears whenever the season ended were all irreplaceable moments that she shared with her "brothers."

"What if the kids on the new team don't want me on their line? What if the coach is mean?"

I felt that knot in the pit of my stomach, too. It started with just a quick glance at my closet. The mountain of purple and black scarves, mittens, and blankets—symbols of friendships built over many years in familiar arenas—would be rendered useless.

Like my daughter, I, too, couldn't help but wonder. *What if the parents are obnoxious? What if the coach is all about winning?*

It's here I had to remember the Great One's famous expression that has echoed through hockey rinks from Manhattan to Manitoba: "You miss 100 percent of the shots you don't take."

Change may be difficult, but if you're always wondering "what if," then you're not willing to take the shot.

Syracuse Nationals mom Jamie Henry was fortunate that her son landed on a team whose parents shared her goals, and the transition was smooth.

"Jonathan's coach held a getting-to-know-you dinner at his house and the kids participated in team-building activities," she said, adding that getting her son to practice early helped give him more time to get to know his new teammates.

"Even though it's only for a few minutes, it really seems to make a difference in forming bonds with the other kids."

Because of his size and position, Duke Holland's 6-foot-3 son draws a lot of attention on the ice, and will use his good nature to help out newcomers to his bantam team by skating with them during drills and sitting next to them in the locker room.

"The big thing is to build confidence, so the quote is, 'nothing negative on the ice,'" says the Kansas City hockey parent. "It's important to offer up praise and leave the constructive criticism to coaches."

Champlin, Minnesota, hockey mom Stacey Christensen also encourages her peewee son to take the lead breaking the ice with new teammates.

"I tell my son to sit next to new players, instead of one of his friends, in the locker room and welcome them to the team," Christensen says.

As for my daughter, she bonded quickly with her new sisters, and the team went on to win tournaments with Sophia wearing the "C" on her jersey. She ended up having what she called "the best hockey season ever."

And it turns out, I looked pretty good in blue and yellow.

various scouts just because of her DNA. She wanted to have that camaraderie that she just wasn't getting with the boys.

Her motivation was far more adult and big-picture-oriented than I ever would have expected for a teenager.

So, the following fall we started a new chapter in our hockey story. Since then, she hasn't really seen too much of a difference except that the locker room is a little quieter, the talk is girlishly foreign for my tomboy. There are also invitations to lunch, sleepovers, and just to hang out, all of which she almost never got before.

For me? I also got to be the new kid on the block.

I spent the beginning of the season trying to fit in with the parents who'd been around for a year and praying that they had compassion for open five holes and fluky puck bounces.

But, hey, I do know some good info about "girly" things.

# 54

## GIRLS LOCKER ROOM VS. COED LOCKER ROOM

### By Sharon Enck

**W**hen my goalie daughter moved from a coed team on which she was the only girl, to a locker room full of other young women, there were bound to be some differences. In our association the hockey moms take turns being "locker room mom," so I have gotten to be a fly on the wall, reluctantly invited into the inner sanctum of girls' hockey-hood. I have to say that some things I've heard were surprising, while others were not.

5. Beauty Tips: While the boys discuss who has the most chest hair, and tease those who have none, the girls are talking about how to remove it. Bonus for me, I got a great tip on which fake eyelashes to buy for my company's black tie gala.

4. Communication: Belching, screaming, and howling have been replaced with an endless, and I do mean endless, stream of chatter about other topics: boys, the

abovementioned waxing, and driver's licenses included. In addition to the endless chatter is an endless sing-a-along to whatever music the DJ has selected.

3. Pranking: No one's bag went in the trash. No part of anyone's gear went in the trash. No one put tape on skate blades and no one was locked in or out of the bathroom.

2. Siblings Permitted: A little sister was actually allowed to be in the locker room and the girls liked it. This would not happen with boys. The sibling would be teased mercilessly until they left screaming "Mom!" in tears.

1. Dress Code: No one had to leave the locker room to change. That's an obvious thing considering the single-sided gender factor. Not so obvious is the "no-girl-left-behind" mentality that goes along with the freedom to change with everyone else.

Some things however do not change. The stink is just as bad (maybe even worse) and apparently farting is still considered high comedy.

Go figure.

# 55

## VALUABLE LESSONS CAN BE LEARNED FROM A LOSING SEASON

**O**ne of the hardest lessons to teach our kids is how to deal with life's pitfalls. That could be because most of us as adults haven't even figured it out.

We all have our tricks for lowering our stress levels—hitting the gym, compulsively shopping, enjoying a glass of red wine. Country singer Zac Brown likes to put his toes in the water, sit back in the sand, and enjoy a cold one.

But sometimes the beach can seem light years away, especially when you're dealing with another tough season. You know what I'm talking about, those emotionally draining campaigns where you've lost track of how many goals your team has surrendered and how many games have been chalked up in the loss column. It doesn't take long before players are losing their confidence, coaches are at a loss for answers, and the parents have lost patience.

*How many more months until baseball season?*

Such was the case during a recent season for Karen Mills Taylor's nine-year-old son.

"Through all this, our son learned that you might not get along with everyone you come across, but you still need to respect them and treat them as you wish to be treated," says the hockey mom from Gonic, New Hampshire.

These tough times not only test a person's character, they also present us with the opportunity to learn some valuable lessons.

"I guide [my son] into discussions about personal and team improvements," says Syracuse hockey mom Traci McLaughlin. "I also remind him that improving is more important than winning."

Michigan hockey dad Mark Gilman says handling a tough season can be summed up in one word—perspective.

"I've had three boys go through hockey, with the youngest now fifteen. They have no memory of wins and losses when they were eight, nine, twelve, or even sixteen," Gilman says. "One of my sons was on a team that won the first game of the year and the last. I'm the only one who remembers this."

It's true—kids don't like to lose. But inevitably, it can be even harder on the parents, who really need to chill.

What if the losing season floods the locker room with negativity? It might be time to talk to the coach and arrange a meeting with players and parents to discuss how everyone should handle the situation.

"Coaches at whatever level—whether they want to or not— are the beginning and end to the locker room environment. It's their responsibility to set the tone," Gilman says.

Joe Wilson, a Colgate University grad currently playing with the Cincinnati Cyclones of the ECHL, says don't let your frustrations start to fester. Confront them head on, and it's better to do so quickly.

"The worst thing you can do is to dwell on it," he says. "The best thing you can do is have that person or 'thing' that can get your mind off the negative."

For Joe, listening to the Zac Brown Band usually does the trick. Suddenly, that beach doesn't seem so far away.

It can be heartbreaking when our kids want to quit. "When Your Kid Wants to Quit"
*Credit:* Darren Gygi

# 56

## THROWING IN THE TOWEL DOESN'T MEAN WAIVING THE WHITE FLAG

Dear Hockey Mom:

I'm having trouble with my nine-year-old son. He's decided he doesn't want to play hockey anymore. I'm crushed. I don't want to force him or push him too hard, but on the other hand, I don't want him to quit. I'm lost and have tried everything I can think of. Please help!

Sincerely,
Heartbroken Hockey Dad

Dear Heartbroken Hockey Dad:

Ah, the dilemma we face as parents. We want to encourage our kids to try new things and have different experiences, but not at the expense of their own happiness or that feeling of "mom made me do it."

Oh how I wish there was a how-to manual for us hockey parents. But what we can try to do is remember the very specific lessons we want our Little Gretzkys to learn. It's not how to dangle through three defenders or feed a teammate from his office behind the net. It's the simple things, like teamwork, persevering through hardships, and finishing what you started.

I remember when my son begged us to sign him up for karate, only to try to bow out three weeks later. We made him finish the six-week trial. He may not have attained that black belt, but he learned a valuable lesson about following through on your commitments. We repeated that lesson with football, basketball, baseball, and the clarinet. It wasn't until he laced up with a stick in his hand that the commitment arguments abruptly ended.

It's important to find out why kids may want to quit. If it's a negative social experience—say, not getting along with a teammate—then it's not so much the sport that's the problem, but the environment. Talking with your child, coaches, and other parents can often help to alleviate some of these issues.

It's also good not to let your kids pigeonhole themselves as just hockey players. Most professional athletes and coaches say cross-training in multiple sports pays big dividends down the road. And at the very least, learning what you don't like can be just as helpful as learning what you do.

One hockey mom—crushed when her son traded a hockey stick for a golf club—bounced back pretty quickly when she saw how his love for the greens got him pumped up in a way hockey never did. It also got him a free ride to a great college. He now has the potential to turn pro.

As hard as it was for them at first, because they were the "ultimate hockey parents," they soon found more joy in seeing their kids discover their passion and potential to succeed at something new and challenging.

Think earnestly about it—what makes you happy as a parent? It's not the tape-to-tape pass or the top-shelf goal, but seeing your kids follow their passion, putting in the time and energy, and ultimately achieving something they previously could not.

And seeing that happen makes any parent know their little one is honestly a Great One.

Sincerely,
Hockey Mom

# 57

## SPORTS PARENTS SHOULD ONLY HAVE FIVE EXPECTATIONS

### By Kevin Duy

**A**s sports parents, we expect a lot out of our kids. I believe that many sports parents make their expectations too high, too unrealistic, and too unfair.

Have you ever had a big expectation that you built up in your mind? Have you ever expected a movie, concert, or restaurant to be so awesome that it was pretty much impossible to avoid being disappointed?

A couple years ago I heard about a certain popular sandwich chain. I remember going online to check them out. The sandwiches looked delicious. I loved the creative concept of the sub shop too. It looked like an awesome place and I was excited to try it out. Unfortunately, at the time there weren't any locations in my hometown of St. Louis. I was bummed.

For some reason, knowing that I couldn't get one in my town, I wanted to it more than ever.

About a year later when our family was on a hockey trip in Nashville, Tennessee, I spotted the restaurant near our hotel. Man was I excited! By this time, I had built up the place so much in my mind. This was going to be the greatest sandwich in the world! I had big expectations.

When we got there, I ordered, filled with excitement. Then it came time to dig into the sandwich that I had been visualizing and wanting for more than a year.

My review . . . "Meh."

The bread was dry. There wasn't enough meat. Too much lettuce.

What a letdown!

The sandwich didn't even come close to my expectations. And even though we have the same chain in locations all over St. Louis now, I haven't been back inside one since. The disappointment was too great.

Or . . . maybe my expectations were too high?

Expectations are a tricky thing. Especially when they come to human beings. More times than not, expectations only lead to disappointment.

For some reason, more and more sports parents are placing ridiculous expectations upon their kids. If you find yourself doing that, stop before you ruin your relationship with your son or daughter.

Don't expect your kid to succeed all the time.

Give him or her the freedom to play freely and without fear of "screwing up." He or she can't play to their full potential or ever get into a flow if they are constantly worried about making a mistake.

Don't expect your kid to be the best player on the team.

First of all, if you put that expectation on your child, then they'll start putting themselves before the team. Games won't be about the team having success, they'll be all about how well he or she played.

Don't expect your kid to get a sports scholarship.

It's amazing how often I overhear other parents of nine-, ten-, and eleven-year-old kids talking about which sports provide the most scholarships. If you're looking at sports as the solution to covering the cost of college, you're placing a heavy burden on the shoulders of your youth athlete. Adjust your expectations and get a new plan.

Don't expect your kid to play pro.

For the love of God, don't ever expect your kid to go pro in their sport. That's all.

## Have Only Five Expectations

From the moment your child puts on a sports team uniform you should only have these five expectations of him or her as an athlete:

### 5. Failure

Your kid is going to fail. A lot. The sooner you not only accept that, but embrace it, the better. I say to embrace it because the last thing you want your child to be is tentative or afraid to mess up. If you've ever played sports, you know that success is never achieved if you play scared.

But guess what'll happen if you jump all over your kid when he or she lets a ball go through the legs, or fans on a shot? The next time he or she gets a chance to make a play, they're going to be thinking about not screwing up instead of just letting the play come to them and executing it.

In a hockey game during a recent season, my then nine-year old son had a partial breakaway. Instead of doing a standard backhand to forehand deke move that he buries about 80 percent of the time, he pulls out "the Tarasenko"—a ridiculous move that St. Louis Blues player Vladimir Tarasenko has pulled off a couple of times in a game.

He failed. Miserably.

He failed and I loved it! He pushed the shot wide of the goal. But everything besides that was awesome. I couldn't believe that he tried it in a game. It would have been a big goal too. His team was down by two at the time.

I didn't care. I absolutely loved that he had the confidence and the creativity to try to pull off a shot like that. Why the heck not man? He's a kid and he should have some fun out there. And if he would have scored, it would have been the goal of the season!

## 4. Sportsmanship

There's nothing I hate to see more than kids throwing a temper tantrum during a game. There's no excuse for throwing equipment or slamming a stick or bat around because something in the game didn't go your way. When the game is over, kids need to congratulate the other team for a good game. No matter how heated a game was, when it's over, it's over. Shake hands and go home.

I had to have a long talk with my youngest son, Carter, after an intense indoor soccer game during a recent season. Carter was really getting into it with a kid on the other team. They had quite a few rough battles for the ball. I saw the other kid take some cheap shots towards the end of the game. He got his elbows up a couple times and kicked Carter from behind another.

I watched the handshake line extremely close after the game. I saw what I was hoping wouldn't happen. Carter twisted the other kid's hand in the line. I was not pleased.

I immediately went over and talked to him about it when he came off the field. He started bawling as soon as I got one sentence out. "That kid grabbed my hand and squeezed it instead of high-fiving me like everyone else!" Carter said as he continued crying. "He was kicking me and elbowing me all game Dad."

"Did you twist his arm in the line?" I asked.

"Yes. When he squeezed my hand I squeezed his back and turned my hand over," Carter said.

I wanted Carter to apologize to the other kid, but I lost sight of where he went after the game. That wasn't a proud moment, but we talked about it for a while afterwards. I think Carter learned a valuable lesson. I'll be very surprised if he ever does anything unsportsman like that again.

## 3. Respect

This one is closely related to sportsmanship, but I feel like it deserves to stand on its own. When kids play sports there are a lot of different elements they should be expected to respect.

Coaches: Kids aren't always going to agree with their coach's decisions, but they always have to respect them.

Officials: Refs and umps are going to blow calls. A kid should never argue or use body language that lets everyone know that he or she didn't think a call was right. They need to respect the call that was made and live with it.

Sports parents need to do a much better job modeling this behavior. (Not you, of course. The other parents on your teams.)

Teammates: No matter what, kids need to support and respect their teammates. They should never point fingers or place blame on other teammates after a loss.

Opponents: If kids don't have respect for their opponents, then bad things can happen quickly in sports. Bad things that can affect another kid's life well beyond one game. These include hits from behind in hockey, head shots in football, hard slide tackles in soccer, a cheap-shot slide in baseball, or an intentional foul in basketball. All of those plays can seriously injure someone. They're all plays that take place when there's a loss of respect.

## 2. Hustle/Effort

I don't know about you, but if my kid's stepping onto a playing surface, he better give his best effort every time out. There's never an acceptable reason for a kid not to hustle. When a kid develops the habit of hustling in sports, it carries over into other areas of life. Always expect your kid to hustle.

Hustle = Hunger

Hunger = Drive

Whatever my kids end up doing in life, I want them to be driven. I want them to set audacious goals and then bust their butt going after them. That begins and ends with Hustle with a capital "H."

## *1. Have Fun*

This one's pretty simple. If you don't expect your kid to have fun while he or she's playing a sport, then why the heck would you have them play? Youth sports are always about fun. The moment your kid stops having fun playing, it's time to find him or her a different team or sport all together.

The expectation should always be to have fun.

# 58

## ON THE NHL BEAT

**E**ver wonder what it's like to be a reporter for the NHL? I was fortunate to connect with NHL.com staff writer Mike Morreale. He is also the author of *The Scholastic Ice Hockey Playbook*, a terrific read for high school hockey coaches, players, and parents. I had a fascinating conversation with Mike about his work, his passion for hockey, and why it's not our imagination that hockey players relish the opportunity to put on a uniform, more so than other athletes.

### How NHL.com's Mike Morreale Got His Start

Prior to joining the National Hockey League in January 2008, I worked for seventeen years covering all high school sports for *The Star-Ledger*, a daily newspaper in New Jersey. While that was certainly a lot of fun, my passion was always hockey, at any level. I really enjoyed reporting on high school hockey and was fortunate to come into contact with many great people. At about the time I applied for the position as staff writer at the NHL, the internet was starting to boom. Print media was becoming obsolete and all the advertising revenue was going into online websites—at least that was what I thought.

Long story short, I got the job and in addition to covering the New Jersey Devils on a game-to-game basis, I've worked closely over the last eight seasons as the league's lead writer for the NHL Draft. It's a lot of fun because it kind of brings me back to my roots as a high school reporter with *The Star-Ledger*, covering all those high school and collegiate hockey players looking to make their mark in the sport they love. I enjoy working with the people at the NHL and dealing with the athletes and executives on a daily basis. Everyone has always been honest, respectful, and informative.

I believe that the hockey player is a unique athlete since he is nurtured and comforted not only off the ice, but on it as well. From the time they were young players, hockey parents were required to wake up in the early-morning hours and travel, sometimes over two hours, to reach a hockey rink. Wherever the destination was, they'd sit there, whether it was a practice or game, and watch their child compete. It's unlike any other sport growing up, because especially in ones where fields are perhaps more prevalent, parents are usually driving kids to practice, dropping them off, and returning to pick them up a few hours later.

Today's NHL players are always thanking their parents for those times. I've never met a hockey player who didn't mention some family member as being a huge part in making their dream a reality.

Q: Everyone knows this is an aggressive sport, but do you think it's time to retire the nasty fighting?

A: This was a question I was often asked as a writer for my college newspaper. I graduated Rider University in Lawrenceville,

New Jersey, in 1990. Back then, I felt that if fighting were abolished completely, I think you would start to see more cheap shots taken. Fighting hasn't been as prevalent in the NHL as it was in the early 1970s. There were rules implemented to help curtail the amount of fights, but, for the most part, it hasn't been an obstacle or distraction to our game. If an opposing player knows that a big, tough player is on the ice alongside a star player or promising rookie, maybe he'll think twice about throwing a cheap shot, raising his stick, or throwing an elbow.

Hockey is an aggressive sport and because of that, bodies will collide and tempers might flare as a result. Fighting has always been a part of the game, but players, for the most part, are respectful of each other.

Former NHL player Brendan Shanahan was once asked, "Is hockey hard?" His response: "I don't know, you tell me. We need to have the strength and power of a football player, the stamina of a marathon runner, and the concentration of a brain surgeon. But we need to put all this together while moving at high speeds on a cold and slippery surface while five other guys use clubs to try and kill us. Is hockey hard? I don't know, you tell me. Next question."

Q: You're the author of *The Scholastic Ice Hockey Playbook: Strategies of a High School Coach*. What's the common mistake our high school coaches make with our kids?

A: I feel high school coaching has really come a long way in ice hockey. You look at the amount of talent coming from the high school ranks and into college and it's pretty impressive. The coaching at the higher levels, in the collegiate ranks, and throughout the United States Hockey League and Canadian Hockey League has also been top notch. Many of those coaches are even offered positions in the NHL once they gain the proper experience behind the bench and that's great to see.

I suppose the one thing that troubles me with regard to some coaching is when that coach fails to put in the time with those players who may not be as talented but could use the extra incentive and motivation. I recall some coaches always relying on the same group of players, all the time. Hockey needs to be fun. It needs to be exhilarating, and players need to learn how to respond in every situation. If they're not given that opportunity at a young age, how will they learn when asked to do so at a higher level?

I understand winning is important on the high school level and coaching that winning attitude comes with the territory, but let's not forget that hockey is also a team game and a team is only as good as the sum of its parts. What are coaches teaching those players that remain out for extended shifts?

I believe it's important for every coach to take time to teach and motivate those third- and fourth-line players. I think it would not only benefit them, but the entire team, as well.

I'm a big believer in the old Japanese proverb that a single arrow is easily broken, but not ten in a bundle.

Q: Sadly, two of the most established ice hockey programs in Central New York have just folded due to costly ice time and dwindling numbers. Do you see this as a trend, nationwide, that this is a sport that continues to contract?

A: It's always sad to hear of US programs having to fold but I don't believe this is a trend. In fact, participation throughout the United States increased from 439,140 male and female players of all ages registered with USA Hockey in 2000–01 to 555,175 in 2016–17. Earlier, in 2012, USA Hockey registered its 100,000th player at the eight-and-younger level.

The NCAA has certainly done its part in developing and preparing our athletes for a professional career in the NHL—32 percent of all NHL players were NCAA alums in 2017. The 2017 Stanley Cup champion Pittsburgh Penguins had fifteen NCAA alums on its 2016–17 roster, the most ever for a Cup winner.

There were fifty-five American-born players selected in the 2016 NHL Draft, including twelve Americans in the first round. Center Auston Matthews, born in California and raised in Scottsdale, AZ, was selected with the No. 1 pick by the Toronto Maple Leafs. Matthews was later joined by Matthew Tkachuk (No. 6, Calgary Flames), Clayton Keller (No. 7, Arizona Coyotes), Logan Brown (No. 11, Ottawa Senators), Charles McAvoy (No. 14, Boston Bruins), Luke Kunin (No. 15, Minnesota Wild), Jakob Chychrun (No. 16, Arizona Coyotes), Kieffer Bellows (No. 19, New York Islanders), Max Jones (No. 24, Anaheim Ducks), Riley Tufte (No. 25, Dallas Stars), Tage Thompson (No. 26, St. Louis Blues), and Trent Frederic (No. 29, Boston Bruins).

The 266 US-born players in the NHL in 2016–17 were born in thirty different states. Leading the way were Minnesota (forty-four players), Michigan (forty-two), New York (thirty-four), Massachusetts (twenty-six), Illinois (fifteen), Wisconsin (thirteen), California (twelve), Connecticut (ten), New Jersey (nine), and Florida (six).

Q: What advice would you give to youth hockey players who dream of someday being in the NHL?

A: Stay the course, always play the game the way you were taught, enjoy the time with your teammates, and, most importantly, have fun. I think it's important to listen to your coaches and always strive to be your best in practice. Practice makes perfect, as we all know, so don't ever take it for granted. Always be humble and respectful of your peers and coaches, and remember to play for the logo on the front of the jersey and not the name on the back.

Q: For parents?

A: Encourage, compliment, and support. No player wants to know how bad they did following a game, whether it's true or not. Constructive criticism is one thing, constant criticism

NHL.com writer Mike Morreale with three-time Stanley Cup champ Duncan Keith. *Credit:* Mike Morreale

is another and it wears on young individuals. Parents need to remember that hockey is an emotional game and that there are moments when coaches will yell, maybe something even directed at your child, but there's usually a purpose behind it when teaching is involved. It's important for parents to teach their kids to be respectful of their peers and the game. Don't boast or humiliate a teammate, a player on the opposing team, or an official. Among other things, that type of conduct will embarrass your child. Last but not least, please don't offer your children cash for goals.

Q: In my years of being around hockey people, I've found them to be earthy, willing to lend a hand, and all-around good people. Have you found that to be the case too, and what about the professional players? Who do you think is a standout, someone who just gets it right?

A: Let me share one of my favorite stories as a writer for NHL.com. Each summer, every player and coach on the team winning the Stanley Cup has an opportunity to spend a full day with the Stanley Cup. The summer after the Chicago Blackhawks won the 2010 Stanley Cup, I had the chance to document the day of defenseman Duncan Keith. I was looking forward to it because Keith would spend the day in his hometown of Penticton, British Columbia. It's just beautiful there.

When Keith arrived at the airport to accept the Cup from Cup Keeper Mike Bolt of the Hockey Hall of Fame, reporters and videographers were invited to join Keith and his family on a shuttle to a few destinations he had planned for that day, July 17, 2010.

When I walked onto the shuttle, Keith saw me and said, "Hey Mike, glad you can make it. Do you need anything?"

I had met Keith just twice prior to this big event—and both times it was as a reporter. The first time I spoke to him was during the 2008 NHL All-Star Game when he was invited to play despite being a rookie.

I took my seat in the back of shuttle and thought long and hard on how Keith could have remembered my name without hesitation. It was baffling. I documented, wrote stories and blogs posts about Keith's big day over the next six-plus hours, and posted then at NHL.com.

At the end of the day, Keith invited friends and family back to his house—a beautiful place that also had a beach looking out onto a picturesque lake. He was doing some follow-up interviews for television and then, before heading back into the house, saw me and stopped.

I thought to myself, *Okay, here it comes. Maybe he's going to tell me how he knows me.* Sure enough, he said: "You know what Mike. I never thanked you."

"Two years ago when I earned a spot in the All-Star Game, reporters were coming over and asking me if I felt I deserved to be there since I was only a rookie. If I told them yes, I'd be cocky. If I told them no, then that might have meant I didn't feel I did belonged there. But when you came over, you just started talking about my season and how great it must feel to be rewarded in this way. And, really, I was relieved. So I just wanted to say thank you."

That said a lot about Keith.

As one of the lead writers for the NHL Draft each season for NHL.com, I'm in contact with many of the future stars of the game at an early age. Each is always very conscientious about their upbringing and how meaningful their parents or guardians have been throughout their career.

Jaret Anderson-Dolan of Spokane in the Western Hockey League was and still is one of the most competitive players you'll find available in the 2017 NHL Draft.

He's a proven leader, conscientious teammate, and very clear on the things most important to him: family and hockey. These are traits he learned at a very young age from two very important people in his life—his parents.

Prior to the 2017 NHL Draft in Chicago, I'll never forget a conversation I had with Anderson-Dolan. I learned during our one-on-one discussion that he and his brother, Dorian, were raised by two mothers, Fran and Nancy. Fran is his biological mother. He told me how proud he is of his upbringing and honored to stand up in the fight against homophobia in sports.

"I obviously don't know any other way of being raised, so for me it was normal," Anderson-Dolan told me. "There's a couple of times where during a game or at school people may look to say something to me but like I've said, I'm not ashamed about it. I believe it's very important that I try and make an impact in the community, as well as on the ice, and I won't shy away from doing that."

It became apparent to me during our conversation that Jaret developed an inner strength at a very early age and family played a huge part in that. He rose above all the nonsense directed at him. It motivated him to reach an even higher level. He would ultimately be drafted by the Los Angeles Kings in the second round (No. 41) of the 2017 draft. He served as an assistant captain for Spokane a second straight season in 2017–18, and continues to excel. He's on target to fulfill a childhood dream as an NHL player.

So, yes. Hockey players are different, and very special.

# 59

## HOCKEY SEASON IS WHINE-DING DOWN

### By Caroline Stanistreet

**I think that everyone** I've talked to in the weeks before the end of a season is complaining, whining, and whimpering about the severe weather they've experienced that year.

All of you hockey moms (and dads, of course) have had the joy of driving your kids to the rinks in the worst conditions possible, and have had to shiver in some bitter cold rinks to support your player during games. My guess is that many of those rinks have broken heaters or perhaps a small warming area or lobbies that don't feel quite warm enough! Meanwhile, your child probably spent some time changing into his or her equipment in a locker room with no heat, and then playing, and then literally thawing out after the game with some hot chocolate or soup.

A fun experience? No way.

Well, I let my dogs out, so to speak, one night and while they did what they needed to do, I looked up at the clear sky, the thousands of brilliant stars, the serenity of it all, then said to myself, *hey, things aren't so bad in life!*

Yes, it's cold, and snowy, and cold again, but I've decided that with spring approaching (sometime, somehow!), we should make this month of March . . . wait for it . . .

Hockey Mom (and Dad) Appreciation Month!

Consider these points, then see if you can release some—or all—of the whining from your system:

- Your child stayed healthy enough this year to play hockey and to finish out the season . . . and I mean no flu, no broken bones, and most importantly, no concussions.
- Your player likely skated three, four, five, or six times per week and was still able to finish his or her homework and maintain a decent GPA.
- Your family was able to afford the following:
  - ➢ Equipment . . . how about that larger pair of skates or a replacement stick mid-year?
  - ➢ Gas . . . I'll say no more about that, except *cha-ching!*
  - ➢ Trips to tournaments, including hotel rooms, meals, and "incidentals"—like that cocktail or three you really needed after that overtime championship game?
- During those trips, you may have had the opportunity to see family or friends you wouldn't normally see.
- He or she had *something to do* almost every weekend, and not sit around and complain that there was *nothing to do* during the winter doldrums.

- Your child secured new friends and maintained the old ones, and maybe as a parent, you made some new friends, too.

- Your kid might have had a tremendous improvement in his game, be it defensively, scoring goals and assists, getting his or her first shutout, hat trick, or MVP award.
- Your kid stayed in reasonable shape for the next sport he or she may play in the spring, be it lacrosse, golf, baseball, or track.

If you're a younger parent, you get to enjoy this all over again next year, where many of us "old" parents might have had our final year of youth hockey.

So, moms, dads, kids, let's appreciate this hockey season for the memories it brought. And as for our winter, it is what it is in our part of the world. Things could be a lot worse and you can always look forward to spring—it is coming!

# 60

## MAKING HEADS OR TALES OF HOCKEY'S ALPHABET SOUP

**For people outside** of youth hockey, AAA is the number you call when your car breaks down. AA puts you on a twelve-step program to sobriety. A is the grade you want on your child's report card.

But those letters have a whole different meaning to hockey parents.

Youth hockey leagues throughout the country are often divided into separate levels of play. Tier 1, or AAA, offers the highest level of competition with more games and typically more travel.

"AAA hockey can be a great environment to play and develop for players who want that challenge. Scouts and recruiters will pay the most attention to the AAA level because, by definition, that's where they will find the largest pool of talented players," according to Nate Ewell, deputy executive director of College Hockey Inc.

Aaron Haider's son Ethan played goalie for the AAA 2001 Minnesota Blades and says, "It has helped him become the goalie he is today."

Diane Firmani made her son wait until he could drive before letting him join an AAA team because of the ninety-minute drive from Wasilla to Anchorage, and the additional fees associated with AAA hockey.

The intensity of AAA hockey can build players and families, but it can also break them if they're not careful. We were careful to budget ahead of time and anticipate the extra cost of traveling and hotels with my daughter's Syracuse Nationals Tier 1, AAA hockey team.

"It's important that families continue to check themselves each season to make sure they are participating in AAA hockey for the right reasons," suggests Jim Sarosy, chief operating officer for the American Hockey League's Syracuse Crunch.

Ewell also points out, constantly trying to "play up" at the highest level can sometimes hurt if a player doesn't get enough ice time or opportunities.

"Honestly, it doesn't make a particle of difference until midgets," Firmani says. "At younger levels, it's merely bragging rights and instant martyrdom for parents."

Minnesota's Champlin Park Hockey Association President Peter Williams advises parents to be smart consumers when it comes to choosing the right league for the player and his or her family.

"Pick a program that has quality coaching, convenient location, and predetermined costs," he says. "If they ask for an open-ended commitment, don't do it."

William's children now concentrate on training and play multiple sports.

Move up the levels—or don't—for the right reasons: for your child, not your ego or your frustrated dreams of professional glory.

And keep in mind NHL.com staff writer Mike Morreale's assessment of hockey alphabet soup, "If you're good enough, you will be found whether it's A, AA, or AAA. Players aren't defined by a letter. They define themselves."

A-men!

# 61

## SHIFTING FOCUS TO STRENGTH AND CONDITIONING

**S**trength is an important aspect in the game of hockey. It's no secret that propers strength training can give kids the tools to be better players and help them win the little battles along with making big defensive plays. It can also help prevent injuries during the season. But what's the right age to get serious?

Certified strength and conditioning specialist Michael Derecola, owner of Strides of CNY, a training center in Syracuse, New York, has compiled training regimens for NHL players and trains high school, junior, college, and youth athletes. He took time out to share advice on how and when to properly train your kids:

Q: Why is strength and conditioning important for hockey athletes?

A: It's important to continue to increase each player's athleticism year-round. In addition, players need to correct any imbalances in order to decrease the risk of injury and improve performance. Increasing strength, power, mobility, and speed are keys in total development of hockey players. This will increase their on-ice skills and skating, enabling them to improve each year.

Q: What age should a parent put their child in the gym and in what kind of program?

A: I believe the age of twelve years is a good age to start training. Start them out in a program that shows optimal coaching with proper lifting and movement techniques. Using body weight exercises then choosing weighted lifts that still allows the player to lift and move with proper form.

Q: What should a parent look for in a program and strength and conditioning coach?

A: The strength and conditioning coach should possess a degree in exercise science or have a degree in a related field. Experience is just also just as important. Finding a strength coach with both should enable to the player to develop appropriately as the years progress.

Q: Have you seen kids maintain their love for training when they start at the right age and with the right program?

A: Over the years, we [my colleagues and I] have trained many athletes. Once the kids see and feel the results, as well as become successful, they understand the importance of strength and conditioning. From there, many have continued to train with us as young adults for they have developed an appreciation for good health, wellness, and fitness. Each year we continue to develop, improve, and advance our coaching and programs to better serve our athletes.

Why not make it a family affair? Moms and dads don't have to sit in the lobby waiting for their kids to get done with their training program. I joined my hockey teens in Mike's gym, gaining their respect, and some muscle, while losing some weight. It was also pretty cool to work out at the same time as some of our pro hockey payers, home during breaks, like NHL forward Alex Tuch!

Resist year-round hockey. *Credit:* Darren Gygi

# 62

## JUST SAY NO: RESISTING THE TEMPTATION OF YEAR-ROUND HOCKEY

In 2016, the great athlete Jim Brown celebrated his eightieth birthday. Most fans know Brown as one of the greatest football players of all time.

What most fans might not know, however, is that Jim Brown may also be one of the greatest lacrosse players of all time. He earned ten varsity letters at Syracuse University in four different sports (basketball, football, lacrosse, and track).

Michael Jordan, the man widely regarded as the greatest basketball player of all time, also starred on the baseball diamond as a kid.

And of course, there's Wayne Gretzky, who was an avid lacrosse, soccer, baseball, and track athlete growing up.

So while it's easy to think practice makes perfect, the truth is diversifying your own little Great One's sports portfolio is actually likely to yield greater returns down the road.

USA Hockey's manager of youth hockey Kenny Rausch is one of the many who can rattle off numerous examples of elite athletes who grew up playing multiple sports.

Rausch says parents should also take into consideration allowing a maturing body to develop properly and in balance.

"Overuse injury is a term we hear way too often in youth sports nowadays," he says. "If you play only one sport you are using the same muscles over and over again. For a body that isn't fully formed, that is a recipe for disaster."

Adirondack Youth Hockey Association's Darryl Coltey thinks that early specialization can stem from parents who are convinced it's the path toward a free ride to college.

"Why does a child have to play a sport for the future?" Cotley asks. "Why can't they just playing for the now? Isn't that what we did when we were growing up? Isn't that the way is supposed to be?"

And lest we forget, anything in excess can cause problems.

For Lonsdale, Minnesota, hockey mom Liz Broske, one word comes to mind: burnout. She encourages her kids to hang up the skates after the season.

"I feel if they were to play all year long, it would become a job to them, and who looks forward to going to work?" she says.

Jim Volpentesta, a hockey dad in Barlett, Illinois, also believes in breaks.

"Otherwise we take our summers off, letting them be a kid for the summer," he says.

Being a kid. Having fun. Playing games—plural.

It certainly worked for kids named Jim, Michael, and Wayne. It can work for your kid, too.

# 63

## REASONS TO LOVE THE OFFSEASON

### By Sharon Enck

**N**ow many of you would argue that there isn't an offseason what with all the camps, clinics, private lessons, and other things parents put their kids through. However I think that even the most hockey-obsessed family can relate to a few of these:

1. Your hockey friends can be just friends again. Maybe you've had too much of each other during the season, maybe they made some disparaging remarks about the goal that deflected off your kid's skate. Either way now you can enjoy each other again.

2. And speaking of friends, you get to see your non-hockey comrades. After all, you have about eight months of catching up to do.

3. The hemorrhaging of money stops, temporarily at least. That is unless you are one of the above-mentioned parents that has their kid in every available camp.

4.  You can talk about other things. For once, you don't have hockey brain 24/7. My co-workers will be most appreciative.

5.  You can take a vacation that isn't a tournament weekend. I know this is a novel concept but you can vacation in places that don't have ice rinks. Yes, beaches are real!

6.  If you're a goalie parent you can finally breathe. It's amazing to me that any of us have brain cells left with the lack of oxygen that takes place when your goalie is in net.

7.  Also in the health department, your blood pressure can return to normal, as there is no threat of a shootout or a close game.

8.  Facebook friends realize that you don't live in a rink and that you have other interests.

9.  The hockey bag stink is somewhat manageable as the gear is allowed to actually dry. Although here in Arizona our overheated garages can bring out some forgotten funk.

10. You can bring in that jacket or parka you've been carrying around in the back of the car. Unless again, you are a camp/clinic parent, then that sucker stays put.

11. Get caught up on your NHL teams and enjoy playoff hockey.

12. Or episodes of *The Walking Dead*.

13. Or your housework (well, maybe not).

14. You get to show off your pedicure! No boots and wool socks, even in the offseason.

15. Enjoy a funk-free car for a little while.

16. Bask in real sunlight, not fluorescent light.

17. Things like hockey tape and game socks cease to be everywhere in your house . . . unless you are one of the moms I know who uses hockey tape for EVERYTHING!

18. Enjoy dinner that isn't overcooked from being in the Crock-Pot too long or grown cold from sitting out on hockey nights.

19. Actually spend time with your spouse instead of being two ships that pass in the night, or in the morning, or in the afternoon.

20. Accept invitations instead of declining because "we have hockey."

21. Spend quality time with your player outside of the car.

22. You don't have to face the school attendance administrative assistant to explain why your player is out of school yet again.

23. Take pictures for your Instagram account that aren't inside a rink, outside a rink, or on the way to a rink.

24. You can kick your feet up with a book.

25. And for you other writers out there, you can write about topics other than hockey because you actually have some time!

# 64

## WHEN IS HOUSE LEAGUE THE RIGHT CALL?

**A**s the movie *Miracle* is required viewing for any and all hockey families, we all know the famous Herb-ism of, "Not looking for the best players, I'm looking for the right ones."

When building a team, Coach Brooks believed it wasn't necessarily about having the most talent, but knowing when, where, and how talent can come together for maximum success. And in order for that to happen, each player on the team must play his or her role—and play it well.

No hesitation. No quips. No complaints.

So what happens when a player's role is tantamount to duster? Are those really the "right" players for a team to have on the roster?

Gregg Kaminski, who coaches Steel City Selects in Pittsburgh, points out that in hockey's purest form, the game is meant to be played for fun, and there's no better way to expose kids to the great sport of hockey than through the house league. In the house league, everyone gets equal playing time, versus travel hockey, where there are cuts and no rules stipulating how much time a player will have on the ice.

"A good house league should also teach the concepts of sportsmanship, hard work, commitment to their craft, how to be good teammates, and the proper way to compete in a healthy environment—and not so much emphasis on winning and losing."

Kaminski says there is no cookie cutter way to advance a player.

"Proper education and exposure by coaches and highly organized/reputable amateur programs help aid this process."

Rob Neimeier—a veteran house coach from Camillus, New York—says you shouldn't underestimate the advantages playing house.

"House leagues can offer a skilled player an opportunity to be a leader where he or she might see limited ice time on a competitive-level squad. The player may inspire or be a mentor for other teammates because they have good physical skills and hockey sense. Those are the players that want to be better."

Whether in-house or competitive leagues, Neimeier says coaches should focus on skill improvement and excellence.

"Fundamentals are largely the same. Drills used by both types of coaches are current and are the best practices that are used by youth, high school, college, and even pros."

Then there are the other factors to consider with house leagues.

"Does the player have the desire to compete at a higher level? Are they willing and ready to commit to the increased practice time, travel demands, and potential for less playing time? Is the player enjoying the house league that provides him or her flexibility to participate in other sports or activities during the offseason?" asks Neimeier.

I've gone through this process before. Not just trying to decide if a house league was right for our daughter, but also dealing with the sting of her being cut from a double-A team.

Not long after though, my family found ourselves playing a game up north. In Lake Placid. At Herb Brooks Arena. AKA, the home of the *Miracle on Ice.*

It's one of my all-time favorite youth hockey memories—the moment our daughter scored the game-winning goal: a top shelf shot that stopped my heart, and melted any lingering feelings about being cut from double-A hockey a year earlier.

It was at that moment I realized what she gained by remaining at the house level.

She got more playing time, more opportunities to dig deep and hustle hard. She took chances, got creative, and got gutsy. She even got named Captain.

The next season began a new journey for the family.

Our daughter decided to take a shot at a triple-A team.

She made it.

Was she the best player? I don't know. But I do know that now, her experiences have made her the right player.

**Be prepared for extra costs if your kiddo does makes a travel team that will likely require a lot more traveling plus the purchase of team-colored helmets, gloves, bag, warm-ups, and jacket.

# 65

## BRANCHING OUT WILL HELP THE ROOTS OF DEVELOPMENT

**When the hockey** season ends, my daughter is ready to lace up her cleats and handle a lacrosse stick. At the same time, I know other parents who fill their children's summers with on-ice skill clinics and more travel hockey leagues.

It left me to wonder: Should my daughter stick to one stick? Am I holding her back? Will her teammates improve more than she does by next season?

Kevin Duy, creator of SportsDadHub.com, doesn't think so.

"I feel that every sport has a season for a reason," he says. "The time spent away from playing an organized sport gives them a chance to miss it. By the time their next season comes around, they can't wait to start going to practices and playing games again. It renews their passion and excitement."

That sentiment is echoed by my daughter's Syracuse Nationals coach Kevin Ahern, a physical education teacher and longtime coach from Oswego, New York. He says no one should underestimate the importance of a child playing multiple sports.

"I can remember not thinking about hockey in the off months, but then getting that refreshed, burning desire to get back on the ice that all truly passionate athletes need," Ahern recalls.

Young athletes not only risk mental burnout, but also physical blowout. Duy's research finds that the repetitive stress on joints and muscles can be eased by engaging in a variety of activities.

"By playing different sports, they're building and strengthening multiple muscle groups that will eventually help them in every sport as they get older and stronger," he says.

But all the science and common sense in the world can't shelter parents from being bombarded by those who claim that stepping away from the rink will slow a child's development or leave them behind another player who plays year-round.

Mark Benedetto, a youth hockey coach in Lysander, New York, changed his way of thinking when he noticed that his sons didn't seem to be having much fun at the rink.

"We put the boys in swimming, lacrosse, fitness training, and golf with less time at the rink," Benedetto says. "We have seen a big difference in their development both physically and mentally. I am a believer now."

That doesn't mean that kids can't enjoy a week at a hockey school or play a little pick-up hockey from time to time.

"As long as they are active and doing something that puts a smile on their face, as a coach I am happy," Ahern says.

As the summer sun rises high in the sky, it is okay to let your kids play soccer, swim, throw a ball around, or, like my daughter, run around a lacrosse field. It will make them happier and be ready to go when they do return to the rink.

# 66

## "I HAVE MET THE ENEMY AND HE IS US." YOUR KID IS NOT AN INVESTMENT.

### By Mark Gilman

**There are probably** not many reading who remember this infamous phrase from a 1971 Pogo cartoon, but many of you hockey parents have had the chance to live out the message. Maybe some of you have actually reached the epiphany that I have.

Recently, I came across an article written by a former OHL Player and now coach, Gregg Sutch, who every day sees firsthand what I just described. That the joy of hockey sometimes is sucked out of the rink by parents looking to enhance their "investment."

Sutch says in part:

> The parents that stand out are the ones who live their dreams through their children. They put their children in every imaginable off-ice and on-ice training camp they can find in the summer, so Little Johnny can make it to the NHL. When Johnny makes it to the NHL, it's all

going to be because of his parents. Johnny is going to repay all the money they've put in for him. Let's stop and take a reality check.

Admittedly I used to be "that parent." My blog had become therapy for me over the years. It's like when I complain about baseball or hockey parents and their behavior to my wife and she rolls her eyes long enough for me to realize I've just described myself. Spouses are like that. Living, breathing mirrors to your ugly soul. Fortunately, it seems as if the more I've written about abhorrent hockey parent behavior, the better human being I've become. Reading about it helps too, like Sutch's well-penned article.

That said, I've chased the golden puck with my kids over the years, looking for the best teams, the best coaching, the best clinics, the best environment for them to go to "the next level." I was talking to a dad last year and asked him if he would have done anything different now that his kid is coming to the end of his youth hockey career. His answer? "I'd have spent a lot less money and not moved around as much." Ditto. I know another father who puts his kid in every possible goalie clinic all summer long and is exasperated by the fact his kid is still the same goalie he was thousands of dollars ago. You can spend money to help define skills. But there is no relation to the money you've spent and how good your kid actually becomes on the ice.

Then there are the parents who shop for "grass-is-greener" scenarios. The best part of Sutch's article was when he stated what we all know but fail to acknowledge:

Now you have kids travelling all over North America to play for stacked AAA teams. Why? Kids are coming from

Florida to play minor hockey in Toronto. Why? Detroit Red Wings star Pavel Datsyuk was found in Siberia. I know it's cliché but, "if you're good enough, they'll find you." It's not fair for parents to take away a childhood by moving to Toronto to play in a hockey hotbed. Besides that, the child doesn't learn a trait that is hard to find these days: loyalty.

He's absolutely right. I live in Michigan where AAA teams, even at the early 12U levels, are stacked with kids from California, Florida, Illinois, and Ontario. Does this mean that Michigan has run out of top-quality players? Hardly. It means coaches are only concerned about winning now, and getting championships and developing nationally ranked super teams, not developing local talent. If your kid is lucky enough to play high school hockey, ask them if any of their teammates ever asked how many trophies their team won when he or she was a bantam or peewee or squirt? Our priorities have been misplaced at best.

One thing I know for sure. Our kids have never initiated a conversation where they have asked to move away to play on a better team, whether it be a local town or to another state or country. It all comes back to our "investment." The thing that concerns me most is what happens when your investment doesn't come through with expected results. Do we think less of our kids for "squandering our money," or do we relish the memories of an opportunity to watch him or her grow, mature personally, and become closer in the parent-child relationship because of the amount of time we've spent together? I hope for all of us it's the latter. Like me, we all tend to get smarter about this the older we get. Measured investments belong on a balance sheet, not a sheet of ice.

Many of you have your feet solidly on the ground (or ice). This is for those who have lost their way and are the first to point to others when talking about the problem with parents in youth hockey. Remember, the biggest issue might be in your mirror. It may quite possibly be "us."

# 67

## QUEST FOR COLLEGE SCHOLARSHIP MAY LEAD TO SCHOOL OF HARD KNOCKS

**You've noticed some** skill in your young hockey player's game, which gets you to thinking—hoping, really—that there could be a free ride to college in the cards.

To bolster your child's chances, you decide to remove all other distractions from his or her life so that he or she can spend all his or her time and energy focusing on your, *I mean*, your child's dream. It makes sense that anything less than a total commitment will jeopardize his or her chances of scoring that sacred scholarship.

Statistically speaking, your dreams are not based on reality, and you could be doing your child more harm than good by stifling their athletic development.

My daughter dials it down when the season comes to an end. This way, she can play other sports, develop new athletic skills, and make new friends while getting a mental and physical break from the rink. One interesting byproduct has been that the time away has been good for the hockey side of my daughter's game.

"It's been proven over and over that cross-training can be helpful for all sports," says Syracuse Mountain Hockey coach Scott Montagna, whose son played Division I hockey. "Let the player have fun, explore, and find their own way. Especially when they're young."

Veteran hockey coach John Katko, from Camillus, New York, also encourages his sons to play other sports.

"To me, the more sports you can play the better," he says. "You develop different muscles, coordination, and skills with different sports, which in the end makes you a better athlete."

The father of a college hockey star and NHL draft pick, who asked to remain anonymous, says his son always played several sports growing up. When the time came to get serious, he still took time away from the rink.

"In the spring and summer, we would cut back to once or maybe twice a week," he says. "Kids need a break mentally and physically from the intense AAA schedule. Parents need a break, too."

Burnout can be a factor, and that's when knowing your kid comes into play.

"An athlete's most valued instinct is desire," says Oswego, New York, coach Bill Cahill, whose daughter plays four sports. "There's no way a child can keep optimal motivation for a sport if they're playing twelve months a year. It becomes a job."

Keep in mind that the numbers are not in your favor. According to USA Hockey registration numbers for the 2013–14 season, there were 61,000 boys and almost 9,000 girls between the ages of fifteen and eighteen playing hockey. Then figure that there are fifty-nine men's programs and twenty-nine women's programs at the DI level with an average of twenty-five roster spots and eighteen total scholarships up for grabs. Add into the mix the number of players from Canada and European countries vying for spots and you're facing some pretty stiff competition.

And one final reminder from the father of that NHL prospect: "The thing I always tell people is I am raising a person, not a hockey player. A sport is just a tool. Using more sports means I have more tools to raise the best person possible."

We need to remember to let kids be kids. *Credit:* Darren Gygi

# 68

## WHAT'S THE RUSH? PUMPING THE BRAKES ON UNREALISTIC EXPECTATIONS.

**When it comes** to athletes—especially the ones who rise to the pinnacle of their respective sports—work and practice are around-the-clock endeavors. Kobe Bryant's drive and workouts are the stuff of legend. Wayne Gretzky famously spent hours honing his skills on a homemade rink in his childhood backyard.

So, it only stands to reason in the minds of many that one should eat, sleep, and breathe a particular sport in order to achieve maximum success. Right?

Well, not quite. There's a lot of science, and common sense, that the opposite is true.

Kobe is actually an avid soccer fan, and grew up kicking a ball around the streets of Italy when his dad was playing professional basketball there. Michael Jordan always played baseball—though not always successfully. Six-foot-three, 300-pound lineman John Urschel, currently the hulking left guard of the NFL's Baltimore Ravens, divides his time between football and advance mathematics. He's currently pursuing his PhD. At MIT, no less.

"If there was a formula to becoming a professional athlete, it would have been bottled long ago," says Jim Sarosy, the chief operating officer of the AHL's Syracuse Crunch, who also happens to be a hockey dad.

Being around peak performers every day, Sarosy harbors no illusions of one day seeing the family name adorning the back of a Crunch jersey. In fact, he actually prefers that his kids don't focus solely on hockey, but rather play a variety of sports.

"It's an opportunity for the child to gain additional experience, meet new people, reset mentally, and use different muscle groups," says Sarosy, who also finds breaks to be beneficial to parents. "I strongly feel a timeout from any one sport to play another is healthy for youth athletes. For parents, it serves as a chance to reevaluate, and often times put into perspective, the goals of having their kids play a youth sport.

Evaluating your kids' athletic goals is a healthy thing for parents to do, according to USA Hockey's director of youth hockey Kenny Rausch, who advocates that kids play at a level where they can have fun and success.

Rausch often asks players and their parents looking to jump to the next level this simple question: would you like to score forty goals or four goals next year?

If the answer is forty (it always is), Rausch says the player should stay at the level where that is the more likely scenario.

"We have a lot of kids who jump to the next level who learn to play 'safe hockey' in order to survive and stay in a lineup, instead of being able to be creative and make plays," he says.

Rausch adds that parents should look for red flags—like a lack of interest in participating and behavior issues—when it comes to deciding whether it's time to pump the brakes on hockey. As they get older, if the school work suffers, that's time to hit the brakes hard.

Perhaps one of the biggest proponents of sane sports parenting is preeminent authority of hockey parents, ESPN anchor John Buccigross.

"I have always been a believer that the best thing for the kids and the family is to play at the local rink," Buccigross says. "Also, my kids always played as many sports as possible, to develop as a total athlete, and have fun doing different things."

No need to force the game down anyone's throat, Buccigross says.

"My credo as a parent was always—I can mess it up more than I can help it."

# 69

## RECRUITING 101

### By Caroline Stanistreet

**Junior year through** the fall of senior year may be an exciting time in your high school athlete's life since he or she may be wondering if they will get the opportunity to play collegiate sports, while receiving a good education. There's an exciting aspect for parents too—scholarship money may be available!

You've probably heard guidance counselors say it constantly about your child's journey through high school: "Start early." They are correct. Colleges are recruiting athletes as early as middle school; yes, middle school! It sounds ridiculous, but it is the reality of today's collegiate sports.

So, what do you do? The sooner you can establish, support, and even promote your student-athlete, the sooner you can form new relationships with college coaches who are continually looking for athletes in your child's particular class year. Do not wait until your child is a senior; many parents have found out the hard way with responses like "thank you for your interest, but our roster for next year is full" or "we only have one spot on the team for next year and it's taken." Get going early, and keep moving!

Here's where the "it takes a village" part comes in. You will find that the more people who are out there helping, the more success you will have in getting your child recruited.

But, before you even consider doing anything, talk with your child's high school coach first. Most of them are realists, and he or she will clearly tell you whether your athlete has the "right stuff" to compete in collegiate sports, and if so, at the appropriate level, be it DI, DII, DIII, NAIA, or junior college.

If you do get the support from your child's coach, ask for a letter of recommendation; also ask for letters from teachers and even the athletic director. Next, visit the NCAA Eligibility Center website and get your child registered. This is a requirement to become a collegiate athlete in the NCAA. Also, look at the NAIA and NJCAA websites (all are listed below), which are great alternatives to the NCAA.

The NCAA eligibility website has a wealth of information for parents and athletes, and it guides your student-athlete along in the process. For a one-time fee, you register your child, who is then given an ID number. That number will be with him or her throughout high school, and it comes in handy when filling out college recruiting questionnaires on each college or university's websites. Those questions vary from school to school, but most will ask for a "NCAA ID#." But, it is up to you and your child to keep information updated on the site, for example, once your child takes the SAT or ACT, the scores must be reported to the Eligibility Center. The NCAA will also provide you with its rules—strict guidelines as to when student-athletes are allowed to contact a coach and in what format, be it email, phone, or face-to-face, as well as when the coach is allowed to contact your child. There are a bunch of what the NCAA calls "periods": contact periods, evaluation periods, dead periods, and quiet periods. These recruitment rules, according to the NCAA's website, "seek, as much as possible, to control intrusions into the lives of student-athletes." So, read and adhere carefully!

Next, hiring a recruiting agency or a sole recruiter is something to consider if your child is looking to play DI. The recruiter's job is to further explain those important recruiting rules and have information on every college, junior college, and university on a single website. These agencies also guide your athlete though the process and provide tips and information to keep him or her on track with recruiting timelines and creating a catchy athletic profile, which make your athlete appealing to coaches. They can also assist with that all-important reality check of whether he or she has the talent to play a collegiate sport, and if so, where and at what level? Yes, it costs money, but if you feel your student-athlete has that much potential, it may be a sound investment.

We found that some coaches appear to rely on recruiters, since they know the information provided by a recruiter is verified and documented. Another benefit is that the recruiter will tell your child directly to keep their social media profiles in check, as coaches monitor them often. It's almost like having another parent watching over your kid!

Ask other parents if they've used a recruiter and how they felt about the experience (and investment), and if they think it's worth it. Keep in mind that the recruiter won't do everything for your child. They will make it clear that your child is the key player when it comes to sending emails, updating profiles, sending videos, and making constant contact with coaches.

My son graduated from high school in 2016 and already had been "competing" against kids for spots on college golf teams across the country for a few years. Roster sizes for collegiate golf teams range from eight to twelve players, or rarely up to fourteen. During the process of applying, my son carefully checked each college roster to see how many seniors there were and looked at each college's areas of study to see if it would be a good fit. He was not just looking for roster openings, but also for athletic scholarship money at a quality school. Surprisingly, we found that many NCAA DI and DII schools do not offer scholarships. (DIII colleges do not have any, yet 90 percent of NAIA schools offer scholarships and the NJCAA also offers scholarships.) Some of the DI schools may just have a single scholarship to hand out each year to a lone golfer. That may not be the case for football, hockey, lacrosse, or other larger team sports, so be sure to research carefully.

Since my son was also a pretty good student, there may also have been merit-based scholarship money out there for him as well; it's important that your child keeps those grades up! If he or she needs to re-take the SATs or ACTs to increase a certain score, then do it. The college's admissions office will tell you that an increased GPA and higher scores on standardized tests can result in more additional scholarship dollars. If your child intends to leave the state, looks at college websites to determine if there is out-of-state tuition vs. in-state tuition. There could easily be an extra $10,000 to $15,000 tacked onto the fee for an out-of-state. Also, make sure your child is well-rounded, meaning that he or she is involved in non-athletic extracurricular and some form of volunteer work. Coaches want to see a kind, caring, and engaged student-athlete, not just a high school jock who only focuses on athletics.

Depending on the sport, you may have to contend with the stigma of being a kid from the XYZ. Take the sport of golf for example. Most southern schools don't exactly search out our talented golfers above the Mason-Dixon Line, believing that Northerners only get to play golf for a portion of the year. My son received a return call from a coach in Florida only to get somewhat snubbed from him because, wait for it . . . he played more than one sport! He also has had to compete with the hundreds, perhaps thousands, of international athletes whose parents send them to the United States for high school. Some will return home after attending prep schools or specialized sports academies, but some will remain in the US in hopes they get recruited by a DI school or even become a professional athlete. It's a lot to contend with, but you need to remain optimistic that there is a great college or university that has a program where your student-athlete can play.

This is where the Oriental rug aspect of this chapter title comes into play. The late Nancy Duffy, a longtime local journalist from Central New York (and mentor to me back in the 80s), first advised me that in order to get into the TV news business, you should "wrap yourself in an Oriental rug and show up at the director's door!" I never forgot that advice; it simply means to separate yourself from the pack, be unique, creative, and clever. Think of different ways to approach a college coach. Consider sending your athletic resume not just electronically, but follow up via express mail or priority mail (yes, the old fashioned way— some coaches may really like that!). And when NCAA rules permit (check that out on their website), it's okay to call a coach. Show your interest and they just might show it back.

If there is mutual interest, then go visit the school. Set up a meeting with the admissions office, take a campus tour, and finally meet the coach. Reading brochures or viewing the college website is one thing, but physically being there makes a huge difference. Prepare questions for the admissions counselor, the campus tour guide, and, of course, the coach. The main objective of these visits is to determine whether your child, the college, and the coach will "click." I still remain in contact with my college coach (and it's been more than just a few years!), and hitting it off right at the start will open the door to a successful experience at the college both academically and athletically. If you don't get an all-around positive feeling from the visit, then consider your "B" or "C" school. Don't get discouraged—there is a "right" school foe everyone.

No one said getting your child recruited was going to be easy, but with a firm commitment from your child and the "village" of family, high school and amateur coaches, friends, and possibly recruiting professionals, it may be worthwhile in the long run.

Thanks to the effort of our son and his "village," we are proud to announce that he signed his National Letter of Intent to play Division I golf.

When undertaking the recruiting process, here are some websites to check out:

National Junior College Athletic Association: www.njcaa.org

National Collegiate Athletic Association: www.ncaa.org

NCAA's eligibility website: www.eligibilitycenter.org

The National Association of Intercollegiate Athletics: www.naia.org

# 70

## IT'S SHOWCASE TIME!

**My family didn't** know what to expect when we headed to Pittsburgh for America's Hockey Showcase. The showcase gives the nation's premiere high school players an opportunity to be scouted by college coaches and prep schools. It can be a springboard to the upper echelon of hockey programs in North America. Five days are packed with over fifty competitive hockey games to give scouts on hand (and watching online) an opportunity to recruit talent on the ice. Representing Team New York, with other high school hockey players, it was my sophomore daughter's first experience and exposure to college and prep school recruiters.

This particular showcase was geared strictly towards high school hockey players who rarely get the chance to be in a recruiter's spotlight.

Our squad was comprised of girls from all corners of the state. St. Lawrence Central High School's Dan Rondeau pulled together a mix of teammates and rivals. My daughter found herself on the same line with girls whose teams they had just beaten in the state championship. Bitter rivals one day, best of friends the next.

"To have high school girls grades ten through twelve meeting each other for the first time in the locker room, thirty minutes before the first game, is a priceless moment for all involved," says Rondeau. "Playing girls from around the country representing their state is something they will always have memories of. The experience may or may not deal to future endeavors for some players, but the memory will last a lifetime."

Team New York didn't win any trophies and there wasn't the flood of scholarship offers that some of us had expected. But, the weekend did open our eyes to highly competitive world of college recruitment and piqued our interest to learn more.

And who better to coach us on the ins and outs of this process than a DI college coach? So with that, I'll turn things over to Syracuse University Women's Hockey head coach Paul Flanagan.

### The Showcase from the College Coach's View

Attending a showcase can be a very positive experience for a young student-athlete. The benefits can be many, including quality exposure to potential prep schools and college scouts. It can also allow them to have multiple ice times at one facility, learn new skills from different coaches, and make friends along the way.

### *Are You the One for Me?*

Selecting the right showcase for your hockey player can be tricky. There are a few important factors to consider when deriving the greatest benefit from your time and your money.

### Geographical Fit

Someplace that isn't too far from home and financially reasonable. The cost to attend in some major cities can be steep when you factor in travel, meals, and hotels.

### Competition

Make sure the competition level is right for you. If you are attending a showcase to improve your play and see how well you match up to other players your age, you will want to be in a competitive environment. Go where you will be challenged, but make sure you are not "over your head" in terms of ability, or at a playing level that is too easy.

### Location. Location. Location.

Plan trips to areas that may have prospective colleges, universities, or prep schools close by to visit during showcase downtime.

### *Parent Prep*

Most showcases have some type of seminar that can be extremely informative for parents, particularly if this is the first time attending a showcase and the process is relatively new. Depending on the age of the student-athletes in attendance, the coaches who are presenting will be prepared to discuss topics that are age-appropriate.

The most popular questions during these semianrs typically revolve around the prep school and college recruiting process, since learning the NCAA rules is important for the high-school-aged players.

Understanding the dos and don'ts can help streamline the process down the road, so ask questions if you're not familiar with the rules and leave the showcase a more knowledgeable parent or player. NCAA coaches can only comment in a general sense and are not allowed to be specific in regards to their school, so be careful when asking questions that are specific in nature.

Asking for advice on balancing school and hockey is always a good question. Asking coaches for a coach's thoughts relative to time commitment, attitude, teamwork, and any other attributes you feel appropriate would also be great questions.

### Showcase Showstoppers?

I think a showcase can only hurt an athlete if he or she hasn't prepared properly both physically and mentally to attend and give it his or her best shot. To go to a showcase because friends are going, or maybe a parent wants to go (but they don't) is just a waste of time and money. Skills obviously matter, but so does work ethic and attitude. I suggest only going if the player is ready to work hard, learn new things, meet new people, and, most importantly, have fun playing the game he or she loves.

### Ready or Not?

How do you know if or when your hockey player is ready for a showcase?

You'll know . . . if he or she is competitive night in and night out and exhibits characteristics that they can't get enough of the rink, they're ready.

***When You Are Ready***

If you've identified a school and program as a place you would like to eventually attend, reach out and contact the coach or their assistants. Share your showcase schedule and your high school coach's contact information.

In your pursuit to play college hockey, don't forget about academics! As one DI coach told me, "the higher your grades, the more doors open."

# 71

# HOCKEY PLAYING AT
# A HIGHER LEVEL

## By Diane Pelton

**T**hey say hindsight is twenty-twenty. If you are like me, you tend to overanalyze every major decision you make, especially if it pertains to your kids and their success. When it comes to deciding on what hockey path to take, the decision can be difficult. Should my son or daughter play junior hockey, or go to prep school? The number of junior programs out there is enough to make your head spin. Prep schools are a great stepping stone both athletically and academically. There are benefits to both, but which is best for my player?

I am not sure whether my husband and I are blessed or cursed to have had the opportunity to have two of our sons play higher-level hockey. At times it can feel like both! Our oldest left high school early and took the prep school path to college hockey. This was great for him, as it gave him many opportunities both on and off the ice. The academics were top notch, and he even learned to row crew! Our advice to him at the time was to choose a school you love without considering the hockey component. I know this sounds strange considering he went specifically to pursue hockey, but injuries can happen and you never know what the season will bring. You have to love the school itself. Prep schools are great because they give academic structure, and provide a level of supervision, while still allowing players to become independent. As it turned out, he also played junior hockey after graduation before moving on to college hockey. (You can play juniors until you are twenty-one.)

Our middle son wanted to graduate from his high school with his friends. He looked at prep schools, but really didn't find a school he felt was the perfect fit. He played on an AAA hockey team until graduation, then moved to the New England area to play juniors. In junior leagues, players often are hosted by a "billet family," and older players often rent apartments. My son chose to rent an apartment with three other players. I was nervous, but I have to say that this turned out to be a great learning experience for him. He learned to grocery shop, cook, clean, do his own laundry, and even held a part-time job—all while training and playing! Talk about time management skills.

You may be asking yourself which is better: prep school or juniors? The answer is that it depends on your player. Our job as parents is to guide our children and help them do the research. The first difficult decision is not where to go, but when. Players can attend prep school as "true freshmen," or as "post graduates," matriculating after graduating from a traditional high school. Gifted athletes can play junior hockey as young as fifteen. Ultimately, it is a family decision, one that depends on the maturity and skill level of your player. My advice? Don't jump the gun. It can be flattering for your player to receive offers to leave home early and play at a higher level, but do some research on the coach and the team. What is their placement record? What will your player's role be on that team? Where will they live? How much will this cost? Also, seriously consider if your player is ready to be away from home for extended periods of time. Along with that, you will need to look at educational opportunities if your player isn't a high school graduate yet. Can your son or daughter keep school a priority while training and traveling? In the end, the final decision has to be theirs, not yours. No matter what path you take, there are no guarantees. Many talented players capable of playing college hockey and beyond will not end up on a roster. Will you make mistakes? Yes. Will you look back on certain things and say, "what if"? Maybe. There will always be highs and lows. Remember, hindsight is twenty-twenty, and life, as well as hockey life, is a journey. Enjoy the ride!

# 72

## SENIOR NIGHT PLANNING

### By Caroline Stanistreet

**If you're the** parent of a high school student-athlete who has made it all the way to "the end," meaning your child is a senior who was not cut from the team, maintained good grades, and kept cool throughout the perils and challenges of the high school atmosphere, then a big congratulations goes out to you as a parent.

Eventually, and perhaps pretty soon, it will be time to think about the end of his or her sports season, and the end of the high school athletic career. You're probably aware of "Senior Night" (or in some instances, Senior Day) in which there are often beautiful, well-planned ceremonies honoring senior athletes' family members who've all contributed to the success of a senior's athletic accomplishments.

A few years ago when I was the parent of a sophomore golfer, I witnessed a lone mother who waited for her sole senior son to get off the bus from his final high school golf match. At the bus circle, she held two balloons and some flowers, so I got out of my car and joined her and rallied some other parents waiting to pick up their underclassmen golfers to join us in the tribute. The senior was touched by his fifteen seconds of fame, and I told myself I would try to honor my son with some sort of recognition when the time came for him. Happily for his senior years, he was in a group of six other graduating seniors and spent a sunny fall afternoon with cupcakes, gifts of embroidered golf towels, and even a gracious opposing team (who lost to my son's team, which always makes the event more enjoyable!).

If you have a high school athlete who is approaching this phase in his or her life, and even if you're the parent of a freshman, here are some organizational tips and suggestions to start, or continue, this fun tradition for your high school senior athlete. If your child plays a sport that does not require the philosophy of "many-hands-make-light-work," perhaps you can still take away some ideas that will help your senior athlete enjoy his final moments of high school sports.

## *Corner that Coach*

Always, always, reach out to the coach first if this not an annual tradition with your school and sport. He or she is usually quite receptive to this event and will likely work with you on some potential dates that will work for everyone involved. If there is already a team parent or team manager, then request that that person act as the liaison with the coach. If, for some reason, you cannot contact the coach (they may not work in the school district), then contact your school's athletic office. (Note: the athletic director always appreciates an invitation and a cupcake too.)

### It's a Date

Review the dates and times to ensure there are no conflicts with other significant school events. Most often, Senior Night will coincide with the last home game, meet, or match of the season. Once booked, write down a tentative itinerary of what will be happening during that special block of time with the seniors.

### Location

On the fifty-yard line of the football field? Standing on the three-meter board? Near the tennis courts? Or in the school gymnasium? Coordinate the spot with the coach, groundskeepers, rink manager, and custodial staff ahead of time. Every sport is different, so even if it's something small like a few picnic tables near the ninth green of the golf course, get the okay if it's the right venue to make it a memorable setting for the seniors.

### Form Your Posse

Put together an email list of senior parents, as well as junior parents who will be interested in carrying on this rite of passage for their child the following year. If your senior athlete is on a large team (football, basketball, track, hockey, lacrosse, etc.), then add underclassmen parents to this list as well. They may want to participate, too. Your child's coach will likely have a contact list which will reduce the time to form a large group email. Parents at some high schools already have an understanding that junior families must spearhead and organize the event so the senior parents don't have to think about it. With some teams, parents are also expected to contribute a small amount of money for the senior gifts, or do some fundraising to offset the costs. Always cc the coach on everything too, as he or she may have some suggestions as well.

## *Knowledge Is Power*

If you are dealing with several seniors, then be certain you know who those seniors are, and don't leave anyone out. Ask the senior parents to email you their own first names as well as the senior athlete's siblings and grandparents. (There is the possibility of an announcer who may read this information, so spell names out phonetically if needed.) Find out where their son/daughter will be attending college (if decided), and if they'll continue on with their athletic career. You can also provide the senior athletes with a profile or survey. Have them turn it in so the information can be announced, or write some of the answers on a poster with their picture.

## *Make Your "Honey-Do" Lists*

Remember, parents DO want to help, so creating a list or a few lists and delegating authority will ease the burden on everyone. Simply shoot out a group email with the lists attached and request a reply to all so everyone's in the loop and no effort is duplicated. For example, one list can be for the food and drinks, plates and cups, and other reception-related items. Then, create another list for buying/making decorations and the set up/take down. You can also make a list for making the gifts for the athletes and collecting money. One veteran senior parent from New Jersey recruited another parent to put together a slide show. If you need to set up a meeting, do it after a practice to make it convenient for everyone and give them ample notice, and after the meeting ends, write a detailed follow-up email in case anyone missed it.

### Crafty Gifts and Décor

Depending on the budget, you can create a simple gift if you cannot purchase something more elaborate. There always seems to be an abundance of untapped talent in parent groups (on my son's golf team, I was lucky enough to have a fellow senior parent who was a professional baker). Or how about using those amazing "artsy" parents to decorate posters or bedazzle picture frames? Or say it with flowers: if this is going to be a larger event with family members, order extra flowers to give to Mom and/or Grandma.

### It's a Family Affair

If there are parents who didn't sign up for anything due to work constraints, travel, or just forgetting and feeling guilty about it, then use them for senior night decorations or set-up. You can always designate a family as "Master Balloon Inflators." Just ask the family to fill up a large trash bag with blown-up balloons, a task they can do while watching TV—it's that easy! Siblings (younger sisters in particular) can also turn out to be the best when it comes to helping, so if you can find some of them to assist with pre-festivity decorating, get them on board.

### The Time Is Drawing Near

Review your itinerary, and be sure to stay in constant communication with the parents on your list as well as the coach. Send reminder emails with the date and time in the subject line, and attach the updated lists.

### *Savor the Moment*

Have your phone and camera fully charged that day, arm yourself with extra tissues in your pocket, and enjoy! The moment will go quickly, but with the right preparation, it will create a wonderful and lasting memory for the senior athlete and his or her family.

# 73

# A HOCKEY MOM'S ENDURING MEMORIES

## By Caroline Stanistreet

**A recent spring** marked the end of an era, the end of a fun and interesting excursion called youth hockey. My son Sean finished his second year as a bantam travel player, thus over a decade of memories on-ice and off-ice have been flooding, or perhaps icing over, in my mind.

So, fellow hockey moms and dads . . . do you remember when . . .

The first year he laced his own skates, then the time came when he said, "I can do it all by myself!" My husband and I waited in line quite patiently for his skates to get sharpened. While waiting, we strategically planned the next time his skates needed sharpening, so we could be first in line at the hockey shop the second it opened. His first time he was checked—scary or what? The first clean check he performed on another player, and you felt some strange satisfaction known as "payback." He'd forget a glove, a helmet, or a skate before a game . . . nothing major! We boiled mouth guards for that "custom fit," which the kids all chew to smithereens anyway.

They played knee hockey in the hotel hallways—until the security guard sent them away. Parents talked in the hotel hallways until the wee hours of the morning—until the security guard sent them away. The moms would plan carpools each week to and from practices and games, often a part-time job in itself but well worth the effort. Your first whiff of hockey equipment left you breathless. For some reason, the kids could never smell it. You visited the opponents' towns so frequently, you could practically visit your favorite breakfast place and order "the usual."

Your child may or may not have had a letter on his or her jersey one year or another, but you still had the extreme satisfaction knowing he or she was a team leader.

The relief you felt before every Halloween because you knew you had a ready-made costume, all thanks to the countless practice and game jerseys lying around. The best part was that the kids would collaborate and do it together, forging a "band of brothers" year after year.

You hoped there was a defibrillator nearby because you were about to witness his very first tournament-championship-shootout-goal attempt and your heart raced like never before. The term "reinventing the wheel" for this hockey mom means year after year of working at the all-important snack bar. You may have asked yourself, "Hmm . . . how does that slushy machine work again?" You would put your kids to work and try to make it "educational" by having them make change. All that while hoping to remember how to refill that blasted cappuccino machine if it ran out.

We'd pass the time with other parents between tournament games by playing "what's the coldest rink you've ever been to?" There are quite a few to choose from! You would head to the hotel pool to sit on a lounge chair and watch your kids burn off even more energy. Moreover, it was certainly nice to get out of the cold for a just few hours.

And today . . . you can look down at all those wide-eyed four year olds, toppling onto the ice in their first tyke fest, then look up at your bantam child and wonder where all the time went.

*Credit:* James DeMarco

# 74

## PUCK HOGS

---

**I**n the early stages of a child's youth hockey career, there are two areas every hockey parent should take into consideration during practices and games: punctuality and selflessness.

When my children were just starting out, it didn't take long for my husband and me to become familiar with what would be an all-too-common sight on the ice. From the youngest ages and earliest levels of the game, we had witnessed more than a few selfish players, a.k.a. puck hogs.

I'm sure you've seen them, too—kids with impressive stick handling and scoring skills, more advanced that the other players on the team. They know it, show it, and make sure everyone else knows it, too. They either "forget," or have no interest in being part of something bigger then themselves: their team. Whether it's out of frustration because other kids are slower and can't catch their passes, or they're driven by incentives from mom and dad, they fail to see the value of an assist. (Just as a note for the parent out there who is unfamiliar with the game, an assist is worth the same amount of points as a goal on the stat sheet.)

Some coaches fall into the win-at-all-costs trap and embrace the kids with a nose for the net. Teaching opportunities about teamwork and the importance of puck movement take a backseat to the thrill of seeing the team ahead on the scoreboard.

The truth is, puck hogs can help a team win. But that mentality can bring a whole team down—way down. Even if it's a winning season, you'll find yourself counting the days until lacrosse, baseball, or track begin.

Rather than just turn the page, so to speak, I decided to fill a bunch of pages with feelings about a season with a selfish player. With the help of my family, we came up with a story entitled *The Puck Hog*. It's the not-so-fictional account of a selfish hockey player named Eddie, who prefers to play for the name on the back of the jersey and not the one on the front. It all came together rather quickly.

My children and husband helped with the story's details and dialogue. My talented sister, Rose Mary Moziak, illustrated the story. We had a ton of photographs from my kids' games that inspired her creation of incredibly detailed illustrations, all done in pencil.

My daughter Sophia was the inspiration for the book's main character, a gutsy girl who adds some ice to fiery scenarios. My son, Joe, is the wise older brother who becomes her confidant and offers sage advice. Eddie's dad comes into play too, rewarding his boy for every goal he scores and encouraging the selfish play.

After *The Puck Hog* was published, I took my teamwork-themed show on the road, making visits to schools throughout New York state. My sister would often join me for a presentation we called "Read, Write, and Assist." It turns out that Eddie, the character who lacks character, was someone many children (in all sports and scenarios) already were familiar with. I've received letters from children across the country—even as far away as Wasilla, Alaska—who have shared their own stories and frustration of dealing with Eddies and were inspired by the way Sophia taught the puck hog that a real star makes everyone shine.

Whether you're playing youth hockey or you spend your days in an office, we all know a puck hog who refuses to pass the puck, or the praise of a boss. Hockey teaches us all—both players and parents—the valuable lessons of team work, commitment, sacrifice, and selflessness. We carry these lessons with us long after we've slipped off the skates or the blanket we wrap around ourselves on the bleachers. Living these lessons makes us better teammates, and more importantly, better people.

And that's what makes hockey such a great game.

# 75

# LIFE, LUCK, AND MENTORS

## By Bill Cahill

**L**ife is complicated; it's full of highs and lows and can be difficult to navigate regardless of your age. If you're very lucky you may meet someone that becomes a friend and mentor, someone to help you navigate life. I'm one of those lucky people. Growing up in Oswego, New York, during the 1970s and 80s, I had many great teachers and coaches. When I started playing hockey as a seven-year-old in 1973 (I had big plans to be the next Bobby Orr), I had heard that there was this guy who played goalie at our local college Oswego State, and that he was on the Olympic team for the 1972 games. A few years later, after pursuing a pro career, he decided to make Oswego his home and started coaching in the Oswego Minor Hockey Association. Little did I know at the time that this guy, Gordon "Pete" Sears, would become one of my teachers, coaches, best friends, and generally just a person who would profoundly influence my life in many ways.

Pete was, and still is, an Oswego legend. He is a former coach who I count among my very best friends; he is a person that I have turned to many times for guidance and advice over the last forty years. When he was coaching in Oswego Minor Hockey and later at Oswego High School, kids looked forward to and hoped to play for him some day. He was also my seventh grade social studies teacher. That year, my class learned a lot about European expansion and explorers like Vasco da Gama, but what I most enjoyed was talking hockey with him after school. Around that time, in 1978, I also started attending his summer off-ice workouts that any kid could go to for free. So from age twelve through my high school years, Pete and those workouts (taken from what the Russians had been doing for years) taught me that your body has no limits, you can endure more pain than you think you can, and that you can always, always, do "one more."

Although he was a multi-sport athlete in high school and college, Pete talked about hockey players like they were from a different planet. He always talked about how you can give a hockey player any task in life and they will figure out a way to get it done. All these years later I feel that he was right, that hockey people seem to have a certain grit or toughness that you don't see in most civilians. It is certainly something I've tried to pass on to the players I have coached over the years, and currently the young ladies (which include my daughter Monica) on the 19U team that I coach today. I have Pete to thank for that mindset and I hope to instill in them the confidence that he gave to me and so many others.

Pete's biggest point of emphasis was always about preparation, both mental and physical. He has a list of several hundred "mind vitamins," many of which we have committed to memory, but one of his favorites is "by failing to prepare, you are preparing to fail." Some of these sayings can be found posted in my classroom today. To Pete, these sayings are not just catchy phrases, but a way of life. How many human beings do we encounter in life that make you want to be a better human being? My friend Pete Sears is one of those people.

Pete's high school practices back in the day were the stuff legends are made of (think the "again" scene in *Miracle*). He felt that if we faced a team that had a higher collective skill level, that conditioning and guts could level the playing field, and he was right. Even though his practices would push you to what you maybe thought was your limit, I don't remember a lot of bitching going on. We would do anything for this man and we just turned our minds and bodies over to him for the molding (something parents and kids don't allow much in the twenty-first century). Very recently, another of Pete's former players told me thirty-five years after he last played for him, "you know how much his opinion means to me, he always believed in me, I would have run through a wall for him and I still would if he asked me too." If you later joined the military and found yourself alone in a foxhole at night, Pete was the coach whose teachings of life and toughness would get you through it. He is also the guy you'd want in that foxhole with you, as to this day he is always there for his former players in any way that we might need him.

Pete actually was in foxholes himself as he served in Vietnam for two years before playing for the 1972 Olympic team. One summer when I was in high school, I signed up to attend Phillips Exeter Hockey School in New Hampshire, where Pete worked for many summers. When he found out I was attending the first session of the summer, he offered to take me there himself. With my parents' blessing, off we went. It was a seven- or eight-hour drive and poor Pete must have thought I was a pain in the butt as I questioned him about everything under the sun during the entire ride. A large chunk of our conversation centered on his service in Vietnam, the things he had seen and his experiences as the point man on daily patrols. He also drew many analogies between being in the Army and playing hockey. The one I remember most vividly is that before his unit saw any combat, there were guys who would really run their mouths and brag about what they were going to do when combat came their way. As it turned out, the guys that ran their mouths were the least useful and courageous in a firefight and the rest of the guys in the unit would avoid those types like the plague because they knew they were likely to get themselves and others killed. Remembering that story as the years went by, I found out Pete once again was right on the money, especially during college when you really don't know anybody else as a new freshman. Sure enough, the guys that would brag about their stats and previous accomplishments usually did not make the team, or if they did, contributed very little. To this day when I encounter someone who feels the need to tell me how great they are, I chuckle and think of Pete. Though I would say by and large that hockey players are the most humble of the athletcs I have come across.

In closing, these are just a few of the hundreds of memories and stories I have of my forty-plus-year friendship with Pete. Not everyone in life is lucky enough to find a mentor or a person that has such a positive impact on them. I am blessed to have wonderful parents and I have been doubly fortunate to have several mentors pass along their knowledge, wisdom, and inspiration to me which helped mold me into the person I am today. None of those mentors have had a bigger impact on me than my friend Pete Sears; I could not be more thankful for his influence and friendship.

# 76

## HOW TO BUST A SLUMP

**Y**ou win some, you lose some. But how good are you at staying positive when the kids are getting smoked every game? The yells get louder and the applause gets softer. When the team is in a slump, parents feel it too.

Phil Simeon, owner and lead instructor of Northern Freeze Hockey in Oakville, Ontario, says youth hockey players are often affected by the moods of their coaches. If players sense a coach's frustration or disappointment, they won't respond well and may even regress in their performance or feel insecure about their abilities. Coaches need to recognize the importance of their influence over youth players. Focus on being positive.

### Simeon Says Choose Words Wisely
### *Don't*

Talk about the team's record, stats, or recent poor performance, if anything you want to distract players from this. Don't overdo it with the positive cheering and motivational speeches; they get tiring when things aren't going well.

## *Do*

Focus on the importance of hard work as a team goal, explain why hard work is important.

Be consistent in what you say, even in tough times.

## Set Goals

- Set simple goals for the forwards. For example, as a group they have to get fifteen shots on net.
- Set simple goals for the defense. For example, they can never leave the front of the net open in their zone.
- Recognize the team's performance against the goals you set, rather than the score of the game.
- Do not set goals for goalies.
- Do some fun drills in practice like "baseball on ice."

## Power of Positive Thinking

Slumps are frustrating for everyone. Losing is not fun. Also, everyone involved needs to be realistic about their expectations. We all want our kids to be great at sports, but it's important to recognize challenging times. Start with finding small successes in performance. Identify what was done well. For example, in a close loss, the team must have done some things well; talk about that point with the team and how to build on it. Let the kids know collectively and individually. Be consistent in your messaging and don't talk about every little thing.

Always recognize and encourage hard work. Boost confidence by telling players what they're doing well. A third of a great performance is based on strong confidence; the other two-thirds are hard work and talent. Confidence and hard work can go a long way even with limited talent.

**Avoid the Past**

You can't necessarily control future performance, but there a couple of keys to maintaining sports' success. Be consistent in what you say, do, and expect from the team. If you get too wound up, or let your guard down too much, you can expect that from your players. Your players read and respond to your behavior, messaging, and attitude. If you get angry, your players will react emotionally. If you are chilling out too much, your players will too. These reactions prevent the opportunity to succeed.

# 77

# THE JOURNEY TO NATIONALS

## Getting There

*By Jennifer Terzini, Liverpool, New York*

Of all the sports my children have played, hockey has always been my favorite to watch. Yes, it's freezing cold (even in August) and we often travel far and play early or late, but it's the one sport that has always captivated my attention. I don't understand all of the intricacies of the game, but what I do know is that my son loves it. Not only has he become a better hockey player over the years, but hockey has also contributed to shaping him into a young man who I can be proud to call my son.

We have been blessed with talented, caring, passionate coaches throughout the years who teach not only hockey skills, but life lessons as well. Whispers of Nationals started during my son Kyle's very first year with his "rags-to-riches" team. He knew many of his teammates only from competing against them through the years. In his mind, he had something to prove and his ego was at work. We grew to love the players and their families. While it was always a long shot, Nationals was mentioned as an attainable goal. Whispers turned to talk.

And talk turned to action. After qualifying for Nationals at States, we had less than three weeks to make these boys' dream happen. Blood, sweat, and tears were shed to make this a reality for them.

As it turns out, we had a pretty amazing place to play, Dallas, Texas, where most of the team had never played before. Dallas is a big, beautiful city that provided the perfect backdrop for memories we'll carry with us forever.

Everything seemed so "official" at Nationals. There were serious-looking men in suits with clipboards evaluating the players, catered meals for important people like officials from USA Hockey, the governing body for organized hockey in the United States, team banners from across the country hung from ceilings, and Nationals apparel flying off the shelves. Kyle's team was nervous. They had lost their first two in tight games to teams that they could probably have beaten on any other given day. After losing the first two, we knew we would not advance to the crossover game, where teams from one pool play teams from another pool. Perhaps it was because there was nothing left to lose, but the boys were "on fire" in their final game. They beat a team from California that had lost only one other game their entire season.

From a mom's perspective, hockey is bigger than just the game played on the ice. Hockey is getting to an ice rink an hour before a game so your child can do off-ice drills with his teammates, tape sticks, suit up, and rock it out in the locker room to their favorite "pump up" tunes. Hockey is traveling thousands of miles in a season, staying in random hotels in random cities on the weekends because that's simply how it's done. Hockey is "killing time" with people who go from strangers to family in a seven-game season. Hockey is watching your child share experiences with young men who he will remember and tell stories about well into his adulthood. Hockey is seeing a passion and fire ignited in your son when he skates onto the ice that is unparalleled anywhere else in his life. Hockey is pride, fear, excitement, and love.

> "This is your moment. You're meant to be here."
> —Herb Brooks

## Living the Dream

*By Pam Bianchi, Liverpool, New York*

In 2015, my son Tommy's 16U hockey team, Center State Stampede, traveled to Plano, Texas, to compete in the Toyota-USA Hockey Youth Nationals. The days leading up to the tournament were exciting! When we arrived at the Dr. Pepper Star Center Arena, the reaction was one of sheer amazement. We were finally at the place we had only seen photos of online. All of the banners were hanging from the ceiling displaying each of the teams across the US that would be representing their state (even Alaska). Only two teams from each state were selected, so it was quite an honor for Tommy's team to be there representing New York.

On the morning of the first game, the line to buy apparel was long, but devoted hockey moms waited patiently to get items for their sons, siblings, spouses, and even grandparents. As the much-anticipated first game approached, the lights on the rink were bright, the mood was positive, and the team was ready to go. Games were going on all around us and just to watch teams from all over the US and experience hockey at such a high level was surreal. These teams were the best of the best in their state for a reason. They were skilled: the skating was fast, the puck was cycled quickly, and players competed hard right up until the end of each game. No one gave up because everyone wanted to win. Each player gave it their all.

If just one mistake was made, the opponent quickly capitalized on it. In the season's previous games, Center State could usually recover from a mistake and answer back with a goal to even the score. But against another state-ranked team, it wasn't so easy. Center State lost its first game to Connecticut by two goals and it's second to Texas by one goal, but won the third game against Orange County, California's number one team. It was a hard-fought, physical game right up until the end. A California hockey mom told me after the game that this was only Orange County's second loss all year.

Even more impressive than that, Orange County was ranked eleventh in the nation. Many parents and spectators said that it was the best youth hockey game they had ever seen. After the game, several of the California parents came over to shake our hands and congratulate us on the team's skills. The other hockey moms from California were very nice and complimented our boys. Center State won against the most challenging team it faced, yet did not have enough points to advance to the semi-finals.

Overall, the trip to Nationals was amazing. To be able to hold their own against such tough competition is something for

Center State to be proud of. It was a wonderful experience for all involved families. The memories will last a lifetime.

## Watching from a Distance

*By Suzanne Kozikoski, Liverpool, New York*

A hockey mom's perspective from another state is a hundred times more nerve-wracking than actually being at the game, but when you have another child that has activities during the same week as Nationals, you have to stay home while sending your significant other on their way. I had some pretty great hockey moms who did go, because you can't always rely on your partner keeping you up to date on games and keeping you posted with pictures throughout the day.

As a goalie mom, I think I see the game differently than that of a player mom. I watch the other team and think, *Do they have the puck, are they in our zone, or do we have defense? Did my son just let in a soft goal, do we have the defense ready, or was that goal just a damn good one that the other team got on us?* I also watch for shots on goal and analyze, *Are we getting as many shots on goal as the other team, or is it lopsided?* With that being said, you can't have parents sending you all that information minute-by-minute because they are watching their child and game.

When I wasn't able to attend Nationals, even though I was updated throughout the games by both a fellow hockey mom and my husband, it was very hard, nerve-wracking, and at times tear-producing, which was not good because I was at work for that one. I would have loved to have been there and watched my boy play at Nationals, but I would not have changed the quality time I spent with my daughter. It was a whirlwind of emotions, not only while they were in Texas, but even in the qualifying games.

You can bet that if we go to Nationals next season, I will be there. Will I be nervous? Absolutely. But I'll still be watching the game where I always sit, on our side, right on the blue line, without moving.

# 78

## THE ROAD TRIP

### By Caroline Stanistreet

**A**s I sit on a plane heading home from a work meeting, I can't help but think about the next time I will head home in a plane.

That will be the time I return from driving my son twelve-plus hours south to his first year away at college. Attending this school is his dream come true, and for me it's going to be tough. He's the last one to go, and while my daughter is also away at school, she's only a half-hour drive due west.

I think of all the time and hours I spent driving them both to a wide variety of activities. With my daughter, it was horseback riding lessons, Irish step dancing classes (thankfully that lasted only a year), swim club, marching band, and high school musicals.

For my son, it was mainly sports: first hockey, a little cross country, then lacrosse, and then golf. That was mixed in with a few years of piano lessons (those I wish he continued, but we can't get everything).

I felt so liberated when the day came that one of them began to drive. But, then I reminisced back to the not-so-long-ago days of careful coordination of carpooling with other hockey moms in our neighborhood. Some days I was "off," and on a few of those off days it saved me from seemingly risking life and limb to get them to hockey practice in rather unpleasant weather conditions (snow of an inch or two per hour with high winds for one). One day, I drove six young hockey boys and six stinky hockey bags in my Chevy Suburban, now topping the odometer at 131,126 miles in the few short years since we bought it.

Chauffeuring my daughter was more entertaining, and certainly less pungent. I would listen to the don't-take-a-breath chatter between her and her theatrical or musical friends about rehearsals and how they thought a show or performance was coming together. The conversations and varied opinions always made me chuckle.

But with both my kids, there were always remnants, or trinkets, of the numerous trips in my Suburban. Hair bands, candy wrappers, broken pencils, coins, golf tees, partially consumed Gatorade bottles, and the occasional missing hockey glove were among the items. Strangely enough, a cell phone was once located in the third-row seat, but was reported missing several days after I brought one of my son's friends home . . . I still can't understand since this kid is a *teenager*!

Well, here I am, just a few short weeks later, on the plane home, and trying to be a brave girl. Just two days before, my son and I took the big road trip south. I did, of course, put a photo album together for him of his life. There is a lot of good stuff he didn't remember as a boy, so it was my job to remind him and to make myself feel better (it didn't work). But he really enjoyed looking at some of the events he barely remembered, and it at least reminded him of the friendships he forged, the places he went, and the smile he always had on his face.

We stopped after eight-plus hours from Central New York at just south of Roanoke, Virginia, as I thought the full twelve hours of driving would be too much for me in one day. I was right, but the truth is that I wanted to extend my time with him as much as possible. It will be difficult, obviously, to repeat that same memorable trip with my daughter, as she will be a mere thirty minutes away (perhaps thirty-seven minutes in the winter). But the pain will be the same. Saying goodbye to my college-bound child reminds me of the same unique pain I had during childbirth. You just can't explain it, but it's a whole different kind of hurt than anything you can really describe.

So during my last hours with Sean, especially during the chaotic, yet scenic, trek through Pennsylvania and mountainous Virginia, I did what any good reporter (though retired) would do: ask a lot of questions to get him to talk.

"What classes are you taking?"

"Hungry?"

"Uh, how do you pronounce the name of that 'singer' again? Wiz Kalifah?"

"I could really go for a beeeeerrr . . . uh, ice cream . . . you?"

"What else can I buy you?!"

"Maybe we can find a driving range near the hotel?"

"Where are your roommates from, again?"

"Hungry?"

"When will you be home? I'll book your flight now if you'd like!"

Just the usual questions.

As my plane continues at 30,000 feet into a bright evening summer sky, the makeup-laden tears have dried on my face, albeit temporarily. I vowed that I won't contact him daily like I conspired to do, as I need to cut the cord quickly for both our sakes. However, I'm going to correspond the old-fashioned way, something both my parents did when I was away, and which I'll always appreciate. I'm sending frequent letters and care packages and maybe some money! My husband suggested I send him gift cards to the southern fast food places around campus, which is a great idea, and an excuse to let him know we are all still thinking of him. Not sure if he will save the letters or notes like I did. Since both my parents are gone, any of their written correspondence is priceless to me now, especially the brief, yet humorous, writings of my father. The note was normally folded three ways with either a crisp $10 bill or a check written with his beautiful prep school handwriting for the same amount. And may I remind you that $10 was a fortune in 1980.

I think my husband and I did our job, and a pretty good one at that. I've discovered that being a parent will never have a retirement opportunity, and that's totally okay with me. I just don't want our kids to ever forget their childhood, their upbringing, and the unconditional love they have always had, and always will. But it's time to let go and let them grow into their own wonderful selves, as incredibly different as they are from being just fifty-one weeks apart (and yes, I would do that all over again).

For those of you who are still carting your kids to hockey practice, play rehearsals, golf and tennis lessons, or lacrosse clinics, cherish every moment because it goes way too fast. It's not a cliché; I'm living it right now. Smell those stinky shoulder pads, pick up the change and the Bobbie pins stuck to the car floor, and hum the tunes the kids would try to harmonize on the car radio together. Those road trips are the best, although the one I just took with Sean to college probably topped my list.

Giving back is the greatest assist. *Credit:* Darren Gygi

# 79

## GIVING BACK MAY BE THE GREATEST ASSIST OF ALL

**It was a** simple enough request: could our Bantam boys swing by a nursing home during a tournament in Northern New York to visit an avid hockey fan?

The hockey aficionado with a long love affair with the fastest game on Earth could no longer travel to a rink. She missed the frenetic pace, the end-to-end action, the crunching body checks, and the passionate cheering from the stands. Was there any chance our boys could bring the game to her?

Without hesitation, the boys were all in. When the jersey-clad teens proudly walked into her sterile, quiet room, it turned out that it wasn't quiet for long.

Hockey quickly took over the room and the conversation. The New York Rangers, Gordie Howe, and Stanley Cup predictions were all part of the non-stop banter. Before their goodbyes, she learned all of the boys' names, their positions, and favorite teams.

Perhaps the boys didn't know just how much that visit meant to her, but we parents knew that simple act of kindness was also an important character-building experience. This was reinforced by the note from the aged fan thanking the boys for stirring up "loads of memories."

Building healthy, active communities through hockey is what drives suburban Chicago hockey coach Charice Wilczynski. For nine years, she has organized the girls at the Glacier Ice Arena to raise money to donate hockey equipment and school supplies to low-income families. They've taught hockey moms how to skate and held clinics for Girl Scouts to encourage them to overcome fears and try something new.

"In a community that is so tight-knit and loving, service is such an important part of youth hockey," Wilczynski says. "It is so rewarding for young children to learn how to enhance and empower the lives of other children and families by donating their time and efforts for a greater cause.

Christie's son's team brings some hockey cheer to an avid fan at a northern New York nursing home.

"It is my greatest hope that I will lead the next generation to become inspired about the passion of service to others."

Whether it's mentoring younger kids, ringing the bell for the Salvation Army outside a local store, collecting food for the local pantry, or visiting a hockey fan in a nursing home, giving back to the community should be the goal for all of our young athletes.

The on-ice skills developed during our children's playing days will only take them so far. But the life lessons they learn and character instilled in them will last a lifetime

Skedsmo-IK 2016 summer camp. *Credit:* Thomas Granerod - SportsNorge.media

# 80

## HOCKEY OVERSEAS: OUR NORWEGIAN ADVENTURE

**knew when** I signed up for the hockey mom gig that the journey would take us to faraway places we had never been, but I never imagined it would take us as far as Norway. An invite came from New York East Coast Education Coordinator Mike Bonelli to travel way across the pond.

Bonelli has family connections to Norway and a deep desire to help grow girls' hockey. So he's been reaching out to hockey moms, like me, to generate some interest. He sold me on the cause and the price was right, so my daughter and I couldn't come up with any good reasons not to explore hockey in a way that was truly foreign to us.

So a few months later, off we went. My travelling cohort consisted of my daughter Sophia, five teammates, their moms, and one spirited, adventurous, winsome grandma who endeared herself to, I think, just about the entire country of Norway.

Our girls spent a week at the Skedsmo ice arena (near Oslo) where they ate, slept, shopped, and skated with Norwegian girl hockey players. The camp, run by Per Henrik Nygaard, also allowed the girls to explore the culture, swim in a frigid glacier hole, and ingest yummy and bizarre things in Norwegian grocery stores, like caviar in a tube and some rather disturbing salty licorice. Experiencing backyard barbecues that saw hot dogs wrapped in tortilla with Sprostek (roasted onions) and freshly picked strawberries with custard was delightful and felt a lot like a good old fashioned American barbeque. The more time we spent with the Norwegian girls and their families, the more we discovered the many things in common, besides a love for the ice. My biggest takeaway was their love for spending time with family. They were gracious and humble about everything.

There weren't enough host families, so our girls roughed it for the week at the rink with cots on the floor and a fridge full of lunch meat, cheese, and bread. Imagine ten girls, minus Netflix and mirrors for an entire week; I'm amazed that I lived to tell about it.

We almost made our teen girls' dreams come true when we found the rink where their big crush played, New York Rangers left wing Mats Zucarello. We missed him by a day, but I hope he found the sweet notes left in his big smelly gloves by giddy girls who got chills when they touched them.

At the end of the journey to the land of forests and fjords, we formed some lasting friendships and rich deposits in our memory banks.

When we got back to the States, our intrepid young travelers were honored even further. These young US hockey ambassadors received Congressional recognition by our local Representative, Congressman John Katko:

Congressional Record
Proceedings and Debates of the 114th Congress, Second Session
House of Representatives

Recognizing the Camillus, New York Girls Hockey Team Hon. John Katko of New York in the House of Representatives

Monday, October 10m 2016
Mr. Speaker, I rise today to recognize the Camillus, New York 16U Girls Hockey Team. This summer, six members of the Camillus Girls Hockey team were extended an invitation by USA Hockey's New York East Coast Coordinator, to help grow girls' hockey in Norway. Sophia Burns, Heather Tanzella, Jessica Smith, Francesca Marsallo, Gabrielle Zollo and Sophia Powless embarked on a trip to Norway and were brought together with other young women from across Norway to bring awareness to girls' hockey.

The members of the Camillus Girls Hockey team spent a week at the Skedsmo ice arena hockey camp with other young female players, under the direction of National Women's Hockey League star Celeste Brown. The girls spent a week promoting girls' hockey and playing hockey, all while making new friends and experiencing the Norwegian culture. The girls' story was featured in *Hockey Norway Magazine* where their hard work and dedication to bring awareness to girls' hockey was recognized.

I am honored to recognize this impressive group of young women who are pursuing their dreams and bringing awareness to girls' hockey.

Further, we received this note of thanks from Georg T. Smefjell from Skedsmokorset, Norway:

As responsible for girls and women's ice hockey in Akershus Ice Hockey Federation, I want to take this opportunity to thank all the hockey moms, the hockey grandmother and players for visiting us at Skedsmo. Such visits from very positive girls from across the Pond is very important as we work to motivate, develop and retain girls in this fantastic sport of ours. We wish you all the best for the rest of the week here in Norway, on your return to the US and the coming season(s). We hope that this exchange will continue and serve as motivation for all.

# 81

## HOCKEY MYTH BUSTING

**A** **well-intentioned hockey** dad told me, "Don't buy big when it comes to skates. Instead, buy the best stick." A $200 stick? *Gulp*! Thank goodness that didn't prove to be true. An inexpensive stick won't cheat your child out of goals. When you're just starting out, bad advice can spin you in all the wrong directions. I teamed up with veteran Camillus, New York, hockey mom Caroline Stanistreet to help set the record straight with her top-ten myth list.

10. Early ice times always happen.
    Fact: This just happens when you're young, or in a tournament.
9. Costly equipment and a huge financial commitment.
    Fact: Hand-me-downs (except skates) are always available, and most teams do fundraising to offset costs. Also, car pool!
8. No time for anything else six months out of the year.
    Fact: It's really only a couple of weeknight practices and a few hours on weekends, but if your kid loves hockey,

is there really anything else he or she would rather be doing?

7. The smell is ever-present.

    Fact: Yes.

6. Hockey parents are not nice and helpful.

    Fact: Most parents are fantastic, but there will always be that one dad who berates his child while he's playing, or that one mom who thinks her child is the only one on the team.

5. All rinks are cold.

    Fact: Most rinks are cold.

4. There are too many injuries.

    Fact: Thanks to modern technology in equipment making, there are fewer injuries. Nevertheless, it's hard to avoid the kid who's at the peak of his growth spurt and decides to do an illegal check from behind. Your coach's instructions on checking and your child's ability to listen and learn to practice and implement techniques are key in avoiding debilitating injuries.

3. It's important for my kid to score rather than skate.

    Fact: Everyone likes his or her kid to score. You can only hope his or her skating and stick-handling skills will develop as he or she does.

2. The mom sitting next to me is still my best friend, even after my kid scored three goals and her kid scored none.

    Fact: There may be a little tension, but hey, like USA Hockey likes to stress, relax, it's just a game.

1. My kid is going to play in the NHL.

    Fact: No (sorry). Yes, there are of course some exceptions, but out of the countless thousands of kids who play, the odds are extremely slim! High school? Very likely. College? A slight chance, but a lot more likely than turning pro.

Those ten facts add up to this: bad advice can cost you plenty, but good advice is more valuable than a tournament hat trick.

# 82

# TEST YOUR HOCKEY IQ

**S**o your little hockey players think they know more about the game than you do? Give them a mental hip check with these fun hockey trivia questions, based on the terrific book *The Rookie Hockey Mom*, by Melissa Walsh.

1. The first US-born NHL player was:
   a) Mike Eruzione      b) Billy Burch
   c) Chubby Checker      d) Charlie Conway

2. Youth hockey teams average how many players?
   a) 8–10      b) 12–15
   c) 14–17      d) 17–25

3. During the mid-nineteenth century, the game was known by several names. In addition to wicket, the game was also called:
   a) Break-shins      b) Blade runner
   c) Slippery disc      d) Pond lacrosse

4. A goal, an assist, and a fight in the same game is also known as:

a) Toothless Trifecta

b) Three Amigos

c) Gordie Howe Hat Trick

d) Putting the biscuit in the basket

5. She "got the biscuit in the basket, five hole" means:

a) She left a snack in her helmet

b) She shot the puck out of bounds and into a spectator's lunch container

c) She scored a goal by shooting the puck between the goalie's pads

d) She left the ice for the fifth time to eat between periods

6. Another name for a hockey stick is:

a) Twig

b) Widow maker

c) Woodwind

d) Wand

7. The penalty for checking with excessive speed is called:

a) Forgery

b) Bankruptcy

c) Christmas shopping

d) Charging

8. What do you call a hockey player who gives 100 percent to the team?

a) Grinder

b) Mercenary

c) Martyr

d) Coach's kid

9. How do you spot a true hockey mom?

a) When a truck passes by, her one-year-old points and says "Zamboni"

b) When asked how old her children are, she responds with birth years instead of ages

c) She brags to other parents how she dangled and deked her way to the checkout line

d) All of the above

10. The Hockey Parent Commandments include . . .
    a) Cheer for all players as thou would have others cheer for thine own
    b) Thou shalt not throw things
    c) Though shalt respect the core spirit of the sport: Fun
    d) All of the above

11. It's mean to refer to a kid as a "duster." True or False?
    True. Like "bender," a player would be very hurt to hear his teammates call him this. It refers to a player lacking skill.

12. "Headman" is a noun. True or False?
    False. It is a verb meaning to pass the puck up the ice to a teammate.

13. If a player "delivers a pizza," his coach is happy. True or False?
    False. Delivering a pizza during a hockey game is to give the puck up to the opposing team leading to a shot against or goal against.

Answers: 1. b) Billy Burch  2. c) 14–17  3. a) Break-shins  4. c) Gordie Howe Hat Trick  5. c) She scored a goal by shooting the puck between the goalie's pads  6. a) Twig  7. d) Charging  8. a) Grinder  9. d) All of the above  10. d) All of the above  11. True  12. False  13. False

This quiz was just for fun and I hope you enjoyed it. The real test is of our ability to help our young hockey players build character while creating positive, lasting memories. When that happens, everybody puts the biscuit in the basket through the five hole.

# 83

## THE TOP THINGS I'D CHANGE IN YOUTH HOCKEY AS A PARENT

### By Mark Gilman

**I**'ve fictitiously and temporarily named myself the "Parent Commissioner of Youth Hockey" for a day, and as "King Parent," I came up with twenty things I'd like to change before the season begins. Some are in jest, others have a bit of an anxiety-ridden bite to them. In all cases, your particular results may vary.

### *Limit the Amount of Top-Level Travel Teams*

My kids have played on them, my kids have been affected by them. My bank account has been bludgeoned by them. The bottom line is that many of these high-level travel teams are no longer "elite." Especially at the younger levels, they've become a source of taking my kid's teammates away with promises of glory. Enough already. Wait until you're sixteen before subjecting your kid and your family to the financial and travel burden this brings. Trust me, it's not worth the car window sticker.

### Place a Limit on Travel Teams in General

Some towns and rinks have five or six travel teams in the same age bracket. Why? You want to know what ever happened to house hockey (where kids not going to higher levels just want to have fun)? They're toiling away in the lower legions of travel hockey where parents are paying, at minimum, twice as much money for the opportunity to watch little Johnny's butt get kicked by higher-seeded teams in the playoffs and tournaments. The loss of house hockey is one of youth hockey's great tragedies, never mind the financial toll it's taken on rinks.

### Bring Back Community Teams

I long for the days when kids who went to school together and played in the neighborhoods together also got to play hockey together. Today, with the advent of travel and crazy parents who believe that the coach located fifty miles away is better than the one ten miles away, we've lost our community teams. The Canadians and the Minnesotans are the only ones who still care about and promote this.

### Ban Goalie Parents from the Rink

They're nuts. They're loud. They're brutish. They don't play well with others and I'm just kidding—I wanted to see if you were still paying attention.

### Require Coaches to Talk to Parents

I've been seeing this and dealing with this for years. In what other sport do coaches decide they don't have to have communicate with parents of kids as young as eight? Just stop it. As parents, we're a necessary evil and our money is paying the rent.

We want our questions answered, no matter how ridiculous they may be. If you're coaching a ten-year-old on a local travel team, you're appreciated, but you're really not so special that you don't have to talk to us.

### Require Financial Balance Sheets Be Given to Parents at Least Twice a Year

I've stopped counting all the youth hockey embezzlement stories that come out every year. It's one of the most unsupervised financial activities in your life and parents are at fault for not demanding accountability. And yes, we'd like to know which of our kids' superstar teammates are being "scholarshipped."

### Keep Agents Away from Kids under Seventeen

Back in the 1980s, agents recruited eighteen-year-old players. But now they are watching hockey games where there are thirteen -or fourteen-year-old kids. "Hey, uh, why don't you send your kid to my camp this summer so I can get to know him a little better. We have an elite group we train each year and I'd love to show him how to get to the higher levels." Meanwhile the "coach" is working our kid to join his "roster" of studs. Be wary. If your kid is a prospect, these guys come out of the woodwork and they're very aggressive. I can name on one hand the kids in the whole state of Michigan who actually "need" representation.

### Fine Rinks That Don't Turn on Their Heaters

I know it's expensive, but at an 8 a.m. practice, an 8 p.m. game, or anything in between, at lease turn those suckers on. For the last seventeen years, I've had to go find the "Zamboni Guy" at least once a week because my wife and the other moms had fifteen blankets around them. The rink management should be penalized financially for cruel and unusual parent treatment.

### Ban Kids from Buying any Hockey Stick More Than $140

I was talking to the owner of a major hockey equipment company the other day and he said that parents who have to have the "new $300 sticks" for their kids are just being suckered by the company marketing them. He tells me, for the most part, hockey sticks haven't changed in eight years. His advice? "Buy the closeouts from last year. They're the same stick. Only the paint has changed."

### Require Referees to Be Evaluated

Coaches get evaluated, so why not refs? I have heard for years that there's just not enough supervisors to monitor their performance. So let the coaches do it! The bad referees stay bad and show up every year. Like teachers, it's about time we evaluated them and not just give them ice tenure. Some of them need to be tossed. So why am I being harder on refs than coaches? Most of our kids' coaches are volunteers.

### Ban Youth Teams from Awarding "C" and "A" Designations

I never understood this one. At the younger ages, we specifically push the kids to play as a team. We keep telling them, "there are no stars" on this team. There are no individuals. Yet some coaches continually set others apart by naming them captains and alternate captains by awarding the "C" and the "A" letters for their jerseys. Enough. Most kids below the age of fifteen (and some over) are monosyllabic at best. Many don't even talk to their teammates, never mind inspire them. The coaches who say "I let the kids pick them" are also kidding themselves. You're setting up a popularity contest in a locker room where there never should be one. The best way I can think of to kill this practice is to adhere to the reason the NHL doles these letters out. The NHL only allows those with a "C" and an "A" to talk to referees, not coaches. Enforce this in the youth ranks and this practice will go away very quickly.

## Standardize Seasonal Start and Stop Dates for Younger Kids

There's no reason an eight-year-old should be playing seven or eight months of hockey a year, but it happens anyway. Either overzealous coaches or overzealous rinks trying to cash another monthly check have made this practice absurd. USA Hockey sets youth standards for just about everything except this. It's time they stepped in and determined the length of a hockey season. If you have to wait four-and-half hours between games, you should also require the kids get a full summer away from hockey. Ending in May and beginning in August is no way to encourage long-term devotion to a sport.

## Ban All Cowbells, Bottles Full of Change, and Air Horns

I saw a great line on Twitter recently that said, "you know you're a hockey mom when you tell your kid to grab your keys in your purse and tell them it's under the cowbell." Funny, however, there's nothing more annoying in a rink than cowbells, change bottles, and air horns. Maybe if the parents knew the appropriate time to use them (not when someone is injured, when you have an eight-goal lead, or the other team gets a penalty, all which I've heard), this wouldn't be such a bad practice. By the way, I know moms in particular who are referred to as the "Cowbell Lady." Do you really want that designation?

### Require Parents to Not Address Their Kid until Four Hours after a Game

This one is self-explanatory and totally unenforceable, but thought I'd throw it in as a reminder. I've been a horrible offender and a world's worst "car coach," so this is for me as much as the rest of you. It's hard to stop and doesn't help anyone. First of all, all the vital "instruction" you're giving will be forgotten by the next game anyway. Secondly, most kids who had a bad or sub-par game already feel bad enough as it is. Remember what Mom said: "if you can't say something nice . . ."

### Make Sure Coaches Play Kids at All Positions Prior to their 12U Year

How many times have we read stories about kids who never played defense until they got to college or the NHL? It's amazing. I have a son who has never played defense and I know kids that have never played a wing or center position. Why? Who knows, but I really don't think a youth coach is qualified to determine what position your kid is best suited for. And, until they play them all—how the heck would you know anyway? It's like telling a baseball player he'll only be an outfielder at the age of ten. Makes no sense in that sport and certainly doesn't in youth hockey. As a disclaimer I know a few coaches who do play their kids at all positions, but they are vastly in the minority.

### Give All Parents the "Just Tell Me How Much to Write the Check For" Fundraising Option

Not all team fundraisers are alike, but some are really bad ideas. Some are just not what we'd do in our private life, so why would we do it for sports? For example, my wife and I personally don't gamble or drink and have an issue with poker and beer nights and asking others to buy tickets for these things; it makes us look like hypocrites. That's just us. I know a lot of folks who look forward to these events. One of my kids was on a team one year where a family donated hundreds of cases of leaf bags that were not even of the biodegradable material now required. They wanted him to go through the neighborhood selling them. We wrote a check and we still have about five-dozen boxes of them in the garage. I am fully understanding of the parents who struggle to meet their ice obligations and need these fundraisers to get through the year and I'm glad they have these options. But for some of us, we'd just like to be given the "write the check" amount to avoid having to take part.

### Eliminate Energy Drinks from the Locker Room

One of man's most useless and harmful inventions are energy drinks loaded with caffeine and sugar. These beverages are heavily marketed towards our kids and it's become a regular rite of passage for them to down one (or two) before they hit the ice. Never mind the nutritional issues, this practice is downright dangerous. Coaches, for the most part, have put the kibosh on this practice, but parents still buy them.

### Require Off-Ice Training for All Kids

Unfortunately, off-ice training for the most part has only been a regular element of hockey for upper-level travel teams. It doesn't need to be. No matter what is planned on the ice, our kids do an awful lot of standing around. If you think ice practice gets kids in shape, you're wrong. We used to call my oldest son the "Ice Dog" for the measures he went to in avoiding any physical exertion during team practices. Off-ice training doesn't have to be expensive. We have a very in-shape parent (who embarrasses all of the rest of us) who leads this twice a week for one of my kid's teams. Surely there's a parent or friend or someone who works at the rink that can lead some running, pushups, jumping jacks, squats, or the like for your kid's squad. It's time for teams at all levels to implement off-ice training into their weekly regimen.

### Any Coach or Parent Who Verbally or Physically Threatens a Referee, Coach, or Player Should be Automatically Banned for at Least the Remainder of the Season

I can't tell you how much of this I've seen personally in the past year alone. It's reached new lows. Parents attacking parents, coaches attacking other coaches, coaches striking referees, parents attacking coaches. If you add that to the regular verbal abuse, it's way out of control. The only way to remove an infection is to cut it out. In other words, extract the problem from the rink. Not just for a game, but for the year. Do this and I guarantee this problem will wane. Maybe, just maybe, it will improve our parent reputation (which isn't good).

# 84

## THIRTY-FOUR REASONS WHY ICE HOCKEY IS THE BEST YOUTH SPORT TO WATCH

**By Kevin Duy**

**A**fter ten years as a sport parent of many sports, I declare that the best youth sport to watch is ice hockey. My journey of being a youth hockey parent began in January 2011. My wife and I currently have four kids, three boys and a girl. Our middle boy Brayden was four years old when he asked us if he could play ice hockey.

At the time, I jokingly blamed our neighbors for getting us wrapped up in this expensive sport. (Now I thank them.) We lived on a cul-de-sac and the kids in the neighborhood all started playing street hockey together. Street hockey quickly elevated to roller hockey.

Once he could inline skate, Brayden got the urge to learn how to ice skate. We took all three boys to a few open skates and they all loved it, especially Brayden. After he got the hang of ice skating, he started asking, non-stop, if he could play ice hockey.

That Christmas his gift from us was a session of Learn-to-Play Hockey at our local rink. Since that moment, the game of youth hockey has been the gift that keeps on giving to our family.

## Absolutely No Clue

I came into the youth hockey world completely clueless. I never had the pleasure of playing ice hockey as a kid. As we walked into the rink for that first Learn-to-Play session, I felt totally out of my element. I wasn't even sure how to gear Brayden up properly.

The rink locker room was packed with other kids sitting shoulder-to-shoulder on benches that lined the walls. Parents were also shoulder-to-shoulder kneeling down in front of each kid to help get their equipment and uniforms on. There were huge hockey bags and gear all over the floor.

## Totally Hooked

Once Brayden was geared up, laced up, and ready to hit the ice, he was smiling from ear-to-ear. He couldn't wait. And once I saw him step out there and skate around, I was hooked. Youth hockey clubs aren't stupid. They make their Learn-to-Play programs extremely affordable. They know that once kids and their parents experience youth hockey, they've got 'em hooked.

## What Makes Youth Hockey So Great?

The thing about hockey is that there are so many different elements of the game that kids need to develop. In other sports there are just a handful of things kids learn how to do during their first season or two playing.

Before we get into hockey, let's take a look at what you see your kids learn how to do during their first year or two playing other youth sports.

### Baseball

In baseball/T-ball kids learn how to catch, throw, hit, field ground balls, catch pop flies, and run the bases. That's about it. Most T-ball and first-year Little League practices are brutal to watch. Most of the kids don't have the attention span required to stay engaged the whole time. There's a lot of waiting around in baseball. Kids end up playing in the dirt or swatting bugs out of the air.

### Soccer

During the first season or two of soccer kids learn some basic foot skills like dribbling, passing, and shooting with both feet. They may also learn throw-ins and how to settle the ball. But that's about it. Most soccer games with four- and six-year-old kids are nothing more than games of herd ball; in other words, all the kids bunch up and kick at the ball and each other.

### Basketball

During the first couple seasons of basketball kids learn the basic fundamentals of dribbling with both hands, passing, and shooting the ball. They may learn different types of shots like layups, bank shots, and free throws, but that's about it.

### Football

In full disclosure, I don't have any experience with youth football, so I'm going off of something you should never base opinions around: assumptions. I know there's a ton of technical skills and knowledge kids need to learn in football. But I'm guessing that from a football parent's perspective, during your child's first season or two of football you see him learn how to block, tackle, avoid tackles, get around blockers, throw the football, catch the football, kick the football, and hold the football while running with it. That's about it.

I imagine watching four- to six-year-olds play football is somewhat similar to soccer. Once they hear "hike" it's a massive game of heard ball where every kid on the other team is trying to get the ball.

## The Hockey Difference
### Hockey Parents See Growth in Every Practice & Game

In other sports kids get better over the course of the season. However, you don't really notice the progression from practice to practice.

Let's be honest. The first year or two that our kids play sports, the games aren't all that exciting. And some hour-long practices can feel like four hours.

Please don't get me wrong. I love every sport and I believe that kids should play multiple sports as long as they can and want to.

But when it comes to being a sports parent and watching your kids develop . . .

### Ice Hockey Is the Most Fun Youth Sport to Watch

When your kids are playing in their first season or two of ice hockey, the practices are more exciting to watch than most games they play in other sports at the same age and experience level.

I was blown away by the rapid growth and skill progression I witnessed during my kids' first couple of years playing ice hockey. I'm not even talking about the growth that occurred over the course of those first two years. I'm talking about noticeable growth and development from practice to practice and game to game.

If you're a hard-core soccer, baseball, basketball, football, or any other sport parent and you're rolling your eyes in disbelief right now, allow me to provide some proof.

I'm going to list all of the different skills kids have to learn during their first couple of seasons playing ice hockey.

I'll start with the first thing kids need to do as soon as they step onto the playing surface, which is a sheet of ice, by the way.

## Skating

In any other sport, the fundamental skill is walking or running. Even if your kid starts a sport at the age of four, if he's fortunate enough to be able to walk and run, he's already been walking and running for three years before he attempts to play the sport.

In order to even participate in the sport of ice hockey your kid needs to be able to stand up on skates and move around the ice. I'm a middle-aged man and I still can't do that very well yet!

Check out these skating skills that hockey parents get to watch their kids develop during their first seasons:

1. Skating in a straight line.
2. Skating fast.
3. Falling down and standing back up. (Yes, that's a skill. And an awesome life lesson.)
4. Turning to the left.
5. Turning to the right.
6. Making tight turns.
7. Doing crossover turns.
8. Turning around and going the other way.
9. Transitioning from skating forward to backwards while facing in the same direction.
10. Skating backwards in a straight line.

11. Skating backwards and turning.
12. Skating backwards and doing crossover turns.
13. Stopping any way possible.
14. Hockey stopping on the right side of his body. (A hockey stop is when they can stop on a dime and spray ice.)
15. Hockey stopping on the left side of his body.
16. Skating backwards and stopping while going backwards.
17. Side stepping.
18. Kicking the puck up to his stick when it's at his feet.

We're already at eighteen awesome things hockey parents get to watch their kids do and we're just on the skill of skating. One aspect of the game! Now, there's a chance that I'm in awe of those eighteen things because I've never been able to do any of them well. Most of them I can't do at all. But either way, those are some awesome skating skills hockey parents get to watch their kids develop.

### *Using the Hockey Stick*

Skating all by itself is an impressive thing for a four- or five-year-old kid to do. But when you put a stick in her hands, ask her to control the puck by stick handling, passing, and shooting it while skating and she stays on her feet. That's taking it up a notch.

The skills you'll see your child develop with a stick and puck include:

19. Forehand shot.
20. Backhand shot.
21. Wrist shot.
22. Snap shot.

23. Slap shot.
24. High shot. (Kids who learn how to elevate the puck can be scoring machines in their first couple seasons.)
25. Low shot.
26. Shots from close in front of the net and in traffic.
27. One-time shots.
28. Carrying the puck on her stick in a straight line.
29. Stick handling the puck while her stick moves from side to side.
30. Stick handling the puck while she skates around obstacles.
31. Stick handling the puck while skating backwards.
32. Stick handling the puck and shooting.
33. Passing the puck.
34. Receiving the pass on the blade of her stick.

## *Getting the Feel*

Most of these skills involve your kid getting the feel of doing something. In order to stop, he needs to develop a feel of how to use the edges of his skate blades on the ice. In order to shoot the puck high and hard, he needs to develop a feel of how to launch the puck off the blade of his stick. Nearly every skill listed above involves getting the feel of moving on the ice.

I believe that's why you see so much progress and development from practice to practice and game to game. Once kids get the feel, it clicks for them and they can all of the sudden go from not being able to do something to being able to do it all the time.

It's so much fun to watch your kid "get it." I can remember those first few seasons watching my three boys learn these skills. It seemed like every practice they were getting the feel for something new.

If you have a child who wants to play ice hockey, but you've never played the sport or you're just not crazy about the idea of him or her playing, I hope this chapter makes you reconsider. Sign your kiddo up for a learn-to-play program and I promise, you'll both be hooked.

Ice hockey is the best youth sport to watch your kids play.

P.S. Don't let the expense of youth hockey cost you and your kiddo an awesome experience. Yes, it's an expensive sport, but it's worth it. If you're like me and need a way to make extra money to afford youth hockey, I can help.

The Skaneateles, New York, girls ice hockey team capped off a perfect 19-0 season with a New York state championship in February 2017. *Credit:* Skaneateles High School

# 85

# THE PERFECT SEASON

When I first began writing the story that would eventually become *The Puck Hog*, I was the mother of hockey fanatics and I wanted to do something good for the game that was giving my children something to feel passionate about and our family a positive focus.

I had no idea the book would be a success. I just had a story to tell and a problem to solve. (And I also had the incredible good fortune to have as a sister a gifted illustrator, Rose Mary Casciano Moziak, who blended my words with her images to create a bit of beautiful magic.)

The years of touring hockey rinks to meet parents and players in the course of promoting the book fed me scores of stories of parents and children, their love of the game, their dislike of the politics, and the stress it puts on family time and budgets. Those stories became the basis for a monthly column in USA Hockey Magazine. Those columns form the heart of this book—my attempt at bringing together years of advice on surviving the hockey life.

I hope you found something helpful in this book. Also, I hope you don't make the mistake of thinking there's a perfect plan to struggle through the long drives to cold rinks, the late dinners, and the never-ending piles of laundry. Perfection off the ice is rare; survival alone is enough.

However, perfection on the ice is possible, so I want to tell you the story of a brilliant season for my daughter's team, the 2016–2017 Skaneateles Girls' High School Hockey team.

My husband noticed something special about Sophia's team on the first day of practice. They had talent, but many teams have talent. He said later that night that they seemed to have a work ethic and a chemistry that we hadn't seen with any team before. The chemistry was all the more unusual because Skaneateles fields a combined team, blending players from another public school district and, when the roster has holes, from Sophia's school, Christian Brothers Academy. Skaneateles Schools Athletic Director Mike Major welcomed Sophia to this team.

This was Sophia's first season in high school competition, and her first action after a yearlong layoff with a meniscus tear. She had always played house team hockey. But we saw the lightbulb go on over her head as she discovered she could skate and play with this team, and she found an important place on the second line. Sophia was "playing up," and playing well.

They began to win and the community began to take notice. Soon, their home games were in the local TV sports highlight packages. (As the only girls' team in the county, their away games were *far* away, too far for TV to follow.) The wins began to pile up.

My husband's observations from that first day of practice were spot-on. Head coach Andy Rozak told one reporter during the season, "We have quite a few girls who can score. The big thing is no one cares who scores the goal. They play very unselfishly." Teamwork, hustle, chemistry, and care for each other—all the things a hockey parent hopes for. It paid off with an unbeaten regular season, wins in the state playoffs, and a 5-1 win over Frontier/Lake Shore Orchard Park in the state championship game. They went 19-0, outscoring their opponents 109 to 13 and piling up nine shutouts. More importantly, the team was also named a state Scholar Athlete team, with a combined score of 93 percent.

Perfection.

It's rare and it's wonderful. It's my hope that when it happens to you and your hockey family—whether it's as long as a season or as short as one line change—you will see it, embrace it, and hold it in your memory forever. Because that's what all the driving, the equipment purchases, the missed family events, the chill that never quite comes out of your bones, and the irreplaceable time together as a hockey family are all about.

A round of stick taps for our 2016–17 Skaneateles Girls High School Hockey players.

The perfect team: Sophie Kush, Alison Weiss, Maria McLean, Johna Halko, Lauren Jones, Kat Lindgren, Katie Halko, Emily Cox, Grace Schnorr, Abby Kuhns, Cecily Kawejsza, Katrina Harter, Anne Rubel, Megan Teachout, Healther Tanzella, Jessica Smith, Sophia Burns, Ioanna Christou, Grace Kush, Campbell Torrey, Caroline Corbett.

# ACKNOWLEDGMENTS

**I**t took a team to write this book and many to thank for the assists. For understanding my long nights at the computer, I'd like to thank my husband John and children, Joseph and Sophia, who inspire me endlessly.

*Thank You Team!*

### SKYHORSE PUBLISHING

Harry Thompson
Veronica Alvarado
John Burns
Joe Burns
Sophia Burns
Sharon Enck
Kevin Duy
Mark Gilman
**SAL MANEEN**
**JIM LAMANNA**
Paul Gasparini
**DAVE BULLARD**
Caroline Stanistreet
Darren Gygi Mark Folsom
Jim Sarosy Chrissie Sarosy
Diane Pelton Kristen Fleet Haag
Farah Jadran
Tim Fox Teri Parks
Mike Bonelli Bill Cahill
Mike Major Andy Rozak
Skaneateles High School
AMY COLCOLOUGH MARTY SICILIA

# GLOSSARY

**AAA, AA, and A:** Nationally recognized as competitive levels of organized hockey, with AAA (Tier 1) being elite competition with a more rigourous schedule.

**Age Classifications:** The following Youth and Girls'/Women age classifications have been established for teams registered with USA Hockey.

Youth teams: 8 & under (Mite), 10 & under (Squirt), 12 & under (Pee Wee), 14 & under (Bantam), 16 & under (Midget) and 18 & under (Midget).

Girls'/Women Teams: 8 & under, 10 & under, 12 & under, 14 & under, 16 & under, 19 & under.

High-school age classification is governed under the same playing rules as the Youth 18 & under (Midget).

**American Hockey League (AHL):** The American Hockey League is a thirty-team professional ice hockey league based in the United States and Canada. It serves as the primary development league for the National Hockey League.

**Attacking Zone:** The zone where the opponent's goal is located.

**Assist:** Attributed to up to two players of the scoring team who shot, passed, or deflected the puck towards the scoring teammate.

**Backchecking:** Rushing back to the defensive zone in response to an opposing team's attack.

**Bar Down:** When the puck hits the crossbar and goes in the net. Also known as Bar South.

**Breakaway:** A player has possession of the puck and there are no defenders other than the goalie between him and the opposing goal.

**Cage:** Metal grid that attaches to the front of a helmet to protect the face. The goal is also sometimes referred to as the cage.

**Center:** An offensive player who takes the faceoff and who usually plays in the center of the ice.

**Change on the Fly**: Substituting a player from the bench during a game without a stoppage of play.

**Duster:** An unflattering term for a player who always sits on the bench and who "collects dust."

**ECHL:** Formerly the East Coast Hockey League (the League changed its name to simply ECHL in 2003), a mid-level professional hockey league with teams scattered across the United States and a franchise in Canada. It is a tier below the American Hockey League.

**Faceoff:** The start of the play. The centers from each team stand at the faceoff dot, the referee drops the puck, and the players compete for control.

**Forward:** An offensive player.

**Goalie:** A player who remains in front of the net and is considered the team's last line of defense.

**Hat Trick:** Three goals scored by a single player in one game.

**Junior Hockey:** Ice hockey competition generally for players between 16 and 21 years old. Leagues are considered amateur (with some exceptions). In the United States, the top level is Tier 1, represented by the United States Hockey League. Tier 11 is represented by the North American Hockey League.

**National Hockey League (NHL):** The big leagues! A professional ice hockey league in North America. Headquartered in New York City, the NHL is considered the premier professional ice hockey league in the world and a major professional sports league in the United States and Canada.

**Offside:** A player on the attacking team enters the offensive zone before the puck, unless the puck is sent or carried there by a defending player. When an offside violation is called, a linesman will stop play. A faceoff is then held at a neutral ice spot closest to the infraction to restart play.

**Power Play:** A power play happens when one team has more players on the ice than the other team as a result of penalties assessed to the team that is shorthanded.

**Tape to Tape Pass:** A perfect pass that travels from the tape on the blade of one stick to the tape of the blade of another.

**Toe Drag:** Dragging the puck along the ice with the end (or the toe) of the stick blade on the ice as opposed to pushing with the bottom edge.

**Top Shelf:** The upper area of the goal, right below the crossbar and above the goalie's shoulders. Also known as "where momma hides the cookies."

**Zero Tolerance:** A USA and Canadian hockey policy that sets standards for officials in dealing with verbal abuse directed to them and in their conduct toward all team personnel. The policy is based on the need for understanding, respect, and cooperation to create a safe and fun environment for hockey.

# CONTRIBUTOR BIOGRAPHIES

**Bill Cahill** is a proud husband, father, and sixth grade teacher for over twenty years at Volney Elementary School in Central New York. He has played and coached hockey since 1986.

**Kevin Duy** is a proud sports dad of four (three boys and one girl). He helps other sports parents fuel their kids' passion for sports without burning them out at www.SportsDadHub.com.

**Sharon Enck** is a nine-season-strong goalie mom to daughter McKenna. When she is not trying to debunk the myth that all goalie parents are crazy, she writes and blogs at www.Sharonenck.com.

**Mark Gilman** is the owner and president of Decus Marketing and Communications and owner of Motor City Hawks Junior Hockey (USPHL) in Detroit.

**Diane Pelton** is an educator and avid hockey fan, who lives in Syracuse, New York, with her husband, Paul, and their three hockey-playing sons, Jake (a goalie), Jimmy, and Joe.

**Caroline (Coley) Stanistreet** was a producer, reporter, and host at WHEN Radio, WTVH-TV, and WCNY-TV in Syracuse. She is a manufacturers' representative for kitchen cabinetry with her husband, Dan, and is a regular contributor for Christie Casciano's Syracuse Hockey Mom's Network. Caroline was—and always will be—a proud hockey parent to her son Sean, who began playing at the age of three.

And huge stick taps for our illustrator!

**Darren Gygi's** career as an artist unofficially began in kindergarten when his teacher, Mrs. Jensen—amazed at the complex rendering created by this very young boy—decided to keep his portrait of a cow for her personal scrapbook. For over twenty years, Gygi has been creating exciting illustration work for publishers of all kinds.